From Misery to Mastery

Journey to Freedom and Empowerment

Ruth Cyster-Stuettgen

First published by Busybird Publishing 2015
Copyright © 2015 Ruth Cyster-Stuettgen

ISBN 978-1-925260-16-8

Ruth Cyster-Stuettgen has asserted her right under the Copyright, Designs and Patents Act 1988 to be identified as the author of this work. The information in this book is based on the author's experiences and opinions. The publisher specifically disclaims responsibility for any adverse consequences, which may result from use of the information contained herein. Permission to use information has been sought by the author. Any breaches will be rectified in further editions of the book.

All rights reserved. No part of this publication may be reproduced, stored in or introduced into a retrieval system, or transmitted in any form, or by any means (electronic, mechanical, photocopying, recording or otherwise) without the prior written permission of the author. Any person who does any unauthorised act in relation to this publication may be liable to criminal prosecution and civil claims for damages. Enquiries should be made through the publisher.

Cover image by: Shannon McDonald
Cover design by: Busybird Publishing
Layout and typesetting: Busybird Publishing

Busybird Publishing
PO Box 855
Eltham Victoria
Australia 3095
www.busybird.com.au

Praise from Clients, Coaches and Mentors

Ruth has a special gift for words and creates magic everywhere she goes. Everything she touches is pure gold. I feel deeply blessed to have her in my circle of friends.
Lisa Fitzpatrick
Soul Purpose and Professional Coach
www.LisaFitzpatrick.com.au

It was a pleasure to work with Ruth. She was always listening and supportive, yet pushed me to take action to reach my goals. The result is that I'm now pushing through my fears and doing it anyway. She is the go-to coach for anyone who needs to get focused, have accountability and support. Thanks, Ruth!
Sharon Anderson
Empowerment Coach
www.manifestingforlife.com

I found Ruth's coaching style to be direct and warm-hearted. Her communication skills are excellent. If you need to super charge your life with clarity and focus, Ruth is a brilliant coach I would highly recommend.

Wendy Ferrier
Creative Soul Coach
www.wildsoulscreations.com

Thanks so much for your very interesting talk and information. You must get a great deal of satisfaction helping these ladies as they deal with their home lives and future. A scary place to be for them and it is wonderful that there are people like you who can help.

Patty Scully
Soroptimist International of the Mornington Peninsula Inc

Some people are simply special. They are filled with enthusiasm for the things they have and want to do, they deeply care about the people around them and make them feel great, and they don't ever, ever give up, filling us with confidence in their convictions. Ruth Stuettgen is truly one of those special people.

Danielle Storey
Million Dollar Relationships
www.daniellestorey.com.au

I really enjoyed myself and as I was driving home, I felt settled, at peace, and after a few weeks of inner turmoil, it was a nice feeling. You obviously have a positive influence, so a big thank you.

Rhonda Caddaye
Swim Teacher, Mum

Dedication

I dedicate this book to my darlings, FF Laura, CB Emily and GB Tim. I stand in humble gratitude that you chose me to be your Mama. Shine only your own light. *Ich liebe Euch.*

To Mum and Dad, thank you for being there for us no matter what; I could not have chosen better parents. *Ek het julle lief.*

Contents

Acknowledgements i

Introduction v

Part One: Looking Back 1

Queen Unplugged 3

Part Two: Looking Forward 61

Chapter 1: Life Lessons 63

Chapter 2: Free Fall 72

Chapter 3: Daily Actions 81

Chapter 4: Emotional Dilemmas 90

Chapter 5: Taking Control 99

Chapter 6: Inner World 109

Chapter 7: Breakthrough 122

Chapter 8: Powerful Support 132

Chapter 9: Your Purpose 142

Chapter 10: Adjust the Sails 151

Chapter 11: Effortless Results 162

Chapter 12: Fast Forward 170

Programs and Offers   **181**

    Offer 1   181

    Offer 2   182

    Offer 3   183

    The Passion Test   185

    A Resource Guide for *Your* Journey   186

    Other Resources   187

    Information Regarding Meditation   188

    My Inspirations   189

    Video   190

Acknowledgements

No book of mine shall be complete without being grateful and acknowledging those circumstances and people that led to penning it. Had I not experienced my life as I did, you would not be holding *From Misery to Mastery – Journey to Freedom and Empowerment* in your hands at this very moment. I am forever appreciative and humble that my journey, thus far, has given me the power and strength to accept what I chose to endure – moments of happiness and moments of sadness. Had it not been for the growing global social awareness of family violence, I would not have had the courage to create this gift of empowerment for other women (and men) in such circumstances.

I acknowledge you, my beloved reader, that you chose to come on this journey with me. Only you are to know the reason for doing so. If it is to seek empowerment to create a new you, I bestow this upon you with my fondest blessings, along with strength, peace and love. If you are to be a catalyst, I humbly ask that you remain aware and vigilant to what's happening around us, and pass my message on to those you feel may need it at some point.

Natasa Denman and Stuart Denman, the Ultimate 48 Hour Author Dream Team – you came into my life just when I needed it, by reaching to me with a warm and caring hand. You planted the seed of becoming an author and change-maker for such a worthy cause. You are the ultimate team when it comes to inspiring budding authors, and I thank you.

To Blaise Van Hecke and your dedicated team at Busybird Publishing, thank you for your support and expertise in publishing my first physical book. I am confident this is just the first of many.

Kevin Howlett, thank you for your perfect photographic skills to make my beauty look so unintimidating by adding a couple of strategic lines. I look wise and more mature!

Les Zigomanis, I loved the way you gently nudged me into action without roaring down the telephone line, which would have made me run a mile! Thank you.

Melissa Cleeman, notwithstanding that you are my first ever editor, you are the most amazing and beautiful person. I am grateful for your honesty and your confidence in me and my cause. I will always remember your first feedback, which led me to consult 'Mr. Google' with an incredible discovery, too controversial to mention herein!

A huge shout out to Shannon McDonald, from Shannon McDonald Photography, for my awesome cover photo. You are amazingly talented; thank you!

Thanks must also go to Ana, from Anadesign, for your incredible designs to match the quotes in my book.

My friend, Sharon Anderson and my niece, Yukiko

Acknowledgements

Mukumoto-Ruthford – thanks for researching some of the resources.

I also want to thank my brother-in-law, Derick Olivier, for his brilliant photography.

I want to acknowledge my 'huge' family. Spearheaded by my mum, Lorraine and dad, Carl Cyster, for your endless love and support, no matter how turbulent my life. There are too many names in my family to mention. Even though you all seemingly and relentlessly tease me, you are proud of me and love me nonetheless (I hope!).

Leaving the most important till last, my children: Laura, Emily and Tim. Thank you for choosing to stick with me as your Mama and for having blind faith in me when we stepped into an unknown future. Know that I will always love you and be there for you. Laura, you are my strength, even though we are not always together – thank you for being so independent. Thank you, Emily, for your great drawing skills. I love your drawing of the Wheel of Life and I love how you love life – it's so refreshing for me. And Tim, thank you for allowing me the time to write while you, at your tender yet wise age of eleven, eagerly offered to do some of the housework and cooking (at least that got you away from the iPad for a bit).

Finally, if I sadly missed anyone, please drop me a line and I will make every endeavour to include you in my next edition, (albeit, only after scrutinising that thou doth deserve the mention here)!

Namaste – I bow to you all.

'The moment you take responsibility for EVERYTHING in your life is the moment you can change ANYTHING in your life.'

– 'Yo Pal' Hal Elrod

Introduction

If you're holding this book in your hand, it is for you. It is right for you; you are meant to read it. You may not know why, just be okay with that. Have you been searching for answers, suffering, struggling, stuck and not known which way to turn? You may just find the answers here.

I dreamed a dream to write a book. I dreamed a dream that came true. I dreamed a dream to inspire other women to create lives they have only ever dreamed of, no matter what their age and background. If I can inspire just one woman to say, 'Yes!' to change her life after reading this, I'll have achieved my goal. Those women who have left behind horrible relationships, searching for their own freedom and empowerment – I hope to be that catalyst for creating their own WOW-Factor in all areas of their life.

In writing *From Misery to Mastery – Journey to Freedom and Empowerment*, I have decided to give up being perfect and would rather be authentic. I was afraid to share my darkest hours with the world, those things that most people never share. Then I came across a few lines in the book, *Absolutely Effortless Prosperity*, by Bijan Anjomi – exactly on the day when I intended to write about my life. The lesson for that day was: 'release all fear, know that I am always filled with and surrounded by unconditional love, and embrace peace'. The decision was made!

For as long as I can remember, I always questioned my place on this earth – why I felt so different, why I was going through what I was, and, lately, shouldn't I be settled at my age, like all my other siblings? Why I am the divorced one in the family, why not someone else?

I have come to realise that in my struggle there was a hidden lesson – to find my voice for myself and for others; to be inspired and to keep moving towards my ideal life and business, no matter how small the steps.

This book is not about blaming myself or someone else, pointing fingers at others, moaning, groaning, writing every gory detail or hating. It's not about instant success, reaching perfection or comparing myself to others who seem to be making it big time. As I am writing this, I am still dealing with stuff and I'm okay with that. If I waited for my life to be just peachy perfect, I would never have written this book. When life is not yet the way you want it to be, fake it until you make it.

Working on our inner-self is a journey – beginning with the end in mind – and holding that big vision. Come back to *From Misery to Mastery* again and again; find bits you can use over and over again. Adapt it to your needs, work on yourself, and believe deeply that you were meant to be here now, in this space, in this

Introduction

time. Have faith that no matter how long it takes, the time will come for that big thing. I want this book to be an easy read for you, to flow easily into your mind. I want the strategies to be simple to understand, no difficult tables or explanations – just picture it in your mind and allow yourself to choose instinctively what you need.

I invite you to read through *From Misery to Mastery* in one sitting if that feels right or come back to it again. Wander through the chapters, flick through the pages and let the right page or words jump out at you. I do that with many books and I find just what I need at the time. If you don't resonate with it from the beginning, fear not, it may just not be the right time.

Millions of women (and men) all over the world have experienced domestic violence or are suffering right now, silently, in those abusive relationships. I suffered and endured in silence for what seemed like a lifetime, until I found the strength and the courage to walk away. It took me a long time to leave, thinking it was the wrong thing to do. I know now that it wasn't. I took myself and my children into safety, away from suffering in silence – putting on a brave front to the world – and smiling when all I wanted to do was sink into oblivion.

I reached the point where I said, *'Enough is enough!'* Unfortunately, many people have not yet reached that point. Even more unfortunately, some may never reach it and will deeply suffer, paying a huge price at the hand of their abuser. A sad event that is very close to my home is an example of that. This devastating news swept across our television screens and newspapers around the country. It involved the loss of a young life at the hand of his father. It brought home to me again, my and my loved ones' safety, with the realisation of how important it is to be vigilant and aware when experiencing such times.

Domestic violence or family violence is a global and silent epidemic. It happens in every country and the signs are mostly almost invisible. The victim learns to put on a brave face to his or her friends, family, and workplace, where no one can even remotely guess what is going on. I know – it happened to me. I was a prisoner in my own skin. Even to be writing this book is a big thing for me. There was a time when I did not want to mention the term 'domestic violence', nor did I want to admit to anyone that I was a victim of DV.

Enough *is* enough! I stand tall (all of 160cm!) and say that I survived it, I walked away and I survived to tell the tale. I am able to say that I stood up and allowed my children to see my strength, and know that their mother is strong and worthy. I am able to say that my leaving paved the way for my children to lead lives of peace and harmony, and know that they have the right to be safe and respected as human beings. I feel secure that I modelled the best way that I know, and I sincerely hope my children will know to treat not only themselves but also others, those they love, with respect and love.

I know that there are women who will never want to talk about it. I was almost one of them. That's okay. It's a choice. I want them to know that they are not alone and there is help if they want it. I want to say to them that they do not have to talk about it openly like I am right now, but there will be someone to listen and guide them in a safe place if they choose. Know that if you are one of them, that you are and deserve to be strong, and you are surrounded by unconditional love.

Introduction

I also know that domestic violence is not something that women and men make up. Everyone is different – they see things and experience situations differently. In my opinion, the abuser often does not admit or see that what they have done is wrong. Can it be that millions of women and men are fabricating or misunderstanding such moments of violence?

Everyone has the right to live a peaceful life, with loving and peaceful relationships – *this is our human right.*

I commend those people who have had the courage to move towards peace and a life without violence. And I commend those people who choose to stay in their relationship; it is a very challenging decision to make, one that I had made many times before finally having the courage to leave. I wish you strength to endure and I wish you safety for yourself and your loved ones. I also wish you courage to speak up about your situation. Ask for help. It is not a crime to ask for help. Be aware. Be vigilant. Be safe. Be loved.

On behalf of those women who lack the courage to admit and talk about it openly, I commit to never being quiet about domestic violence. The whole world is behind you! I fully support White Ribbon Day on 25th November, which is the United Nations' International Day for the Elimination of Violence Against Women.

I swear never to excuse or remain silent about violence against women.

I have made it my mission to help those implement powerful strategies to help them move forward with confidence and calmness, to allow them to make healthy decisions for themselves and their families.

Part One
Looking Back

Queen Unplugged

'Adversity will surface in some form in every life. How we prepare for it, how we meet it, makes the difference.'

– Marvin J Ashton

I am about to open up the window of my life to you. Please deal with it carefully; I do not share this with just anyone. I am sharing it, not to burden you, but to show you that I managed to turn my experiences into life lessons to serve me. Let it inspire you.

It all began on a Sunday in March, the year 1965. Sunday children, I've heard, are meant to be special. Coming into this world in the home my father built, 'Forest Lodge', was a feat in itself (this helped me in making my decision to have my last two children at home). I am the fifth child of seven. I say 'of seven', because my oldest brother, Alec, though he was born early, didn't quite live long enough to make a life for himself. He was born prematurely and lived for only a couple of hours. This was, understandably, a very sad time for my parents.

I grew up in a small village called Pniel (meaning, 'The Face of God'), in South Africa. I can't remember much of my childhood, so I'm going to do my best to relay my story here. I believe my story defines my life. Between my birth and the age of five, I can't recall very much.

I started school at five years of age. Apparently, I was ready to start, so my Mum said. Who knows, maybe I was being a pest and she needed to get me out of the house? One day I'll get her to admit it!

I went to school in the neighbouring town, Stellenbosch. I'm not quite sure why, as we did have a school in the village where we lived. I think it was something to do with the month that I was born. Come Monday morning, I would walk to the bus stop as a very unwilling protégé, with an older girl, Fileda.

I didn't want to go on the bus and I would resist as much as possible. Everyone still laughs at this picture in their head of trying to put me on the bus as a five-year-old. You can imagine what that would have looked like! I think I held onto the railings on the inside of the bus door. I put my feet against the steps and resisted. Because of my size, I guess I didn't have a choice and eventually I had to get on. Apparently, I was uttering words that would be extremely inappropriate here. Where on earth would I have learnt such expletives and what a scene that would have been! Thank goodness iPhones and iPads hadn't been invented then, otherwise the video-clip would have gone viral in no time. I can see it now: 'Five-year-old stops traffic' or 'Five-year-old gets mouth washed out with soap by entire village'.

So then, I would stay with the Africa's (the family's surname) and go to school there. On the Friday, I would go back home to my family again. I only spent weekends and school holidays at home in my first year at school, which, I guess, defined my life in some way, as well.

Living with Aunty Rosie Africa and her family was special, despite the fact I was away from my own family. At dinner times we would say 'Grace' and sometimes it was my turn to lead the prayers. The, 'For what we are about to receive, our Lord, make us truly thankful for Christ's sake, Amen', became the 'Our Father, who art in Heaven' prayer. This was, of course, a lot longer and, being said by a five-year-old, didn't help hungry tummies at all! My family still remembers and laughs about that.

From pre-school age to the age of sixteen, I was part of the Girls Brigade, which is similar to the Girl Scouts. It was in this little village and was a big part of my life. It had a religious aspect to it, as well. It was a very enriching experience; it gave us girls a sense of belonging. We had regular events that we attended and it set many of us up for life in how to live in a spiritual way. The Brigade still exists in some parts of the world.

I was a marching girl. We had choreography and marched with batons or sticks, usually in some sort of a parade. At certain times of the year there would be a big celebration, a big carnival, with floats and everything, and the marching girls would be out and about as well. I loved it!

A big part of my childhood was spent playing 'house' – without Barbie or Ken or a complete kitchen/play house. My siblings and I usually grabbed something from our real kitchen: cans of things and utensils like spoons, knives and plates. We'd improvise by collecting things from outside and have fun for hours on end. We were forced to be very creative in our playing, especially since my family wasn't well off. We were a big family and weren't endowed with lots of toys.

We also played 'theatre'. We'd get together with other children in the neighbourhood, and make up our own theatre production. The production was staged in my family's garage, which was re-invented with curtains, a stage and an auditorium. The audience paid a couple of cents to see it.

I climbed trees all the time. I still have the scars on my knees to prove it! My siblings and I had to share one bike with my brother. We lived at the foot of the mountains. We used to ride his bike down this hill outside our house and down the road. Everybody played on the road back then. At the bottom, there was a big fence made of bushes, and sometimes, if we weren't able to brake hard or fast enough, we would then end up in them. That was *a lot* of fun! We would also end up with a few scratches, of course! As well as sharing one bike, we also had one family car.

We used to roam the streets during the day and so did the neighbourhood dogs – the days before dogs had to be on leashes! As soon as we got home from school or if it was school holidays, we'd get up in the mornings, have breakfast, and then disappear outside. Everything was safe; there were children everywhere and we played with each other (whether we liked the other or not). Nobody had to be driven anywhere to visit their friends, as it happens these days. We'd stay out until we were called back in for lunch or dinner.

One pretty cool thing we used to do is get old tires

from cars and used two sticks, one on each side of it. We'd use those as a car. We played games with many different things: pebbles, balls, skipping ropes, sticks and empty cans. My other love was netball. I started playing when I was in primary school and I continued to play until I left South Africa at sixteen.

I attended three primary schools and three high schools. Academically, I was always towards the top end of the class. I had a bit of a healthy competition going on with a cousin of mine, Juliet, who has sadly passed on now. We'd see who was top of the class and who was second or third. Outside of school, we played together.

There were times when Mum chased me around the kitchen table, because I took too long to get the potatoes or other groceries from the shop. I think I had gone to the shop and forgotten about the time or gotten side-tracked playing. That ended up with me being in big trouble.

We would sit around the open fire during winter, eating nuts and mandarines. On Friday nights, 'Derry', my dad, would go out and buy some chocolate (he still loves his chocolate). We'd devour the goodies whilst telling ghost stories at night. No one wanted to go to bed, especially the younger ones. After listening to a ghost story, who was willingly go to bed on their own? Not me!

There were times when we ate or stole fruit from the neighbours' gardens. In Pniel, just about every garden had an abundance of fruit trees. Some people had more trees than others, and we would go into their gardens and help ourselves.

We had lots of fruit trees in our own garden. There were

grapes, loquats (small yellow/orange fruit with large brown pips), oranges, lemons, apples and peaches. That was a very special time of my childhood, just being able to go and eat fruit off the tree. Best taste ever!

We used to have parties, where lots of family and friends came over. The adults would clear the lounge room of the furniture or push it all aside completely. They'd clear up the carpets and play music, dancing the night away. We'd watch the adults dance and learn how to dance ourselves. Thanks, Mammie and Derry for those memories!

My grandmother lived to her nineties. Her white hair springs to mind, along with her walks up the street to the local shop. She did this ever so slowly, with her hands behind her back. We used to call her 'Mama Henna' (Henna for Johanna), while my grandfather was called Papa. They were my dad's parents. Papa was very sick towards the end of his life. When we visited him, he was lying in his bed. I would have been a teenager or maybe a bit younger during this time.

I don't have very many memories of my mother's parents. Her own mother died young, when I was very little, so I don't really know her. My older siblings would know her better. Unfortunately, my mum never knew her dad.

I had my moments of fame as a child. As well as performing in the theatre in the family garage, I also took part in a theatre production run by some talented people in the village. I even had a main singing part that I still remember today. Lord knows how I managed to get a singing part! It goes like this:

'Mama goes here and Mama goes there, Mama goes

out and everywhere, but poor Papa, poor Papa, he goes nowhere at all. When Christmas comes, Mama gets the most expensive frock, Papa gets a necktie, and a pair of Ackerman's socks. Mama goes here, and Mama goes there, Mama goes out and everywhere, but poor Papa, poor Papa, he goes nowhere at all.'

It's amazing that I can still remember that song after so long. I was famous for a very long time with the locals, as well as my 'Papa' partner. I must look him up one day. Who knows, he might have gone on to become the side-kick to Fred Astair!

My baby sister, Edith, suffered a mild form of epilepsy, which she has, thankfully, outgrown. The two of us shared a bed. Back then, we didn't have a room of our own – there were too many kids. Nowadays, just about every child has their own room. So I watched my darling sis's back at bedtime, when she wasn't well. I'd alert Mum and Dad if something went wrong. Edith had her own way of letting me know – she'd pinch me! I think the bruises have gone now ...

My dad had a shoe business he ran from home, which explains the reason for my shoe fetish. It was great having access to all different kinds of shoes. It was something that he tried as a sidekick to his carpentry job. Great combination, right – shoes and carpentry!

As well as having a large family, we also had servants. There was Mrs Krediet, who used to come and help my Mum, and there was another lady, Katy. Both used to help sometimes when we had big parties. It was quite a clever idea; my parents didn't have to stand in the kitchen all night, preparing food and washing the dishes. Instead, they could tend to their guests. There was also Ragel, who came from one of the farms and a gardener, James, who slept in the shed at the back of our property.

We were fortunate to have our milk delivered. We'd have to leave the empty milk bottles outside. There was a holder attached to the brick fence at our front gate. When the milk was delivered, the empty bottles would be exchanged in the holder.

As a teenager, I did the taboo thing of driving a family member's car without permission. I can't remember whose car it was. I think it may have been my brother-in-law's. What I do remember is it was sitting in the driveway and no one was around, so I decided to take it for a spin. The key would have been in the car – no one locked their cars at that time. Houses were generally left wide open, doors unlocked.

I reversed out of the driveway and out onto the road. I was old enough to have an idea on how to drive. Once I got onto the road, my dad drove up – sprung! Panic set in and as I tried to drive back into our driveway, I promptly drove into the wall of the house! Needless to say, I was in a bit of trouble over that.

The family used to go camping by the beach every single year, at Harmony Park after Christmas. We'd stay there for weeks at a time during the summer break. We usually camped on the same spot every year and the same people from Pniel would be there. In the early days, we were in tents, but later on my dad built his own 'cabin'. He would dismantle it at the end of each trip and packed onto a truck. The man had the vision back then! Those times were special. They were spent playing at the beach with older siblings or other kids. The adults were usually back at the campsite, having their own fun.

A rather traumatic part of my childhood is, I guess, the consequences of the apartheid regime that I was born into. Apartheid = segregation = racial discrimination.

My parents weren't born into apartheid, so they remember how life in South Africa was before it was introduced by the government. What I'm about to share is from my own perspective, my memories and what I have heard from other personal experiences. I have not dug into any facts or figures, or gone down the halls of history.

Basically, there were the whites and then there were the non-whites, which were classified into different sub-categories. These were the Blacks or the Natives, the Indians, and the Coloureds. Depending on the colour of your complexion, you had certain privileges. I was classified as a Coloured – a Cape Coloured, because I was born in the Cape Province in the south-west of South Africa. My identity card was stamped with this. I think there was even a letter in front, like on your passport. The identity card had a letter C – C for Coloured. My birth certificate was stamped and classified as my being Cape Coloured or Coloured. I was branded.

The apartheid had far-reaching effects. White people had the most privileges, then, I think, the Indians, then the Coloureds and then the Blacks. The areas where people could live were also segregated. You would never find blacks living in white areas, for example, unless they were employed by white people. The Coloureds lived in one area, the Blacks lived in their area, and then the Indians congregated. I think the Indians and the Coloureds tended to or could mix.

When I was in primary school, I didn't feel the effects of it. We lived in a small village and were pretty much cocooned in. We weren't really openly affected by apartheid, except for when we went out of the town. For example, when we used to go to the shops, whites would get served before blacks, or non-whites. Public places, like toilets or cafés and restaurants, had separate entrances for the different races. Trains had different carriages for whites/non-whites. The first rows on buses were for whites. Beaches were segregated so that the nicer beaches were for the whites and the not so nice beaches were for the non-whites. These beaches could be right next to each other, flowing into each other, but from a certain point onwards, they were totally separate and inaccessible.

School systems were different – different curriculums were taught and different books were used. The riots started from the sixties onwards, and when I was in mid-high school, it escalated. I was pretty prominent in my school as prefect. Our school was heavily involved in the riots and I was part of it. When the riots started, police were called in to put a stop to it. They came into the school grounds as well. There was a time where we protested in the city area, and the police came and put a stop to that too – and not too gently, I might add. We did not protest violently, but it became violent when the armed forces were called in. Some of the protesters ran for safety. If you couldn't, you'd be injured and/or arrested. I escaped both. It was a very scary time for me when I was in it, but I did it for the good of all of us.

Unfortunately, my school was closed down due to these riots. We had to stop classes, close down and go home. When the school was finally allowed to reopen – it took a while for this to happen – my parents had to sign a declaration that I wouldn't partake in any further riots. My parents weren't willing to sign it, which I'm grateful for now, because they stood up for their rights and mine. The downside of it was I couldn't go to that school anymore.

My first part-time job as a teenager was at KFC. I could take some of the leftover chicken home at the end of the night. When I left that job, we had to chase up my last pay from the manager – we never did get it. My dad and I reminisced about that not so long ago. I didn't work there long, as we left for Australia around that time.

My mother and father wanted to give us kids a better future. They didn't see this happening if we stayed in South Africa. The decision was made to immigrate to Australia, with the three youngest children, which included me. My oldest sister was already living in Australia and my other two were married. Our family home, which my dad had built with his own hands, was sold to his sister. We flew out on Christmas Day in 1981. I was sixteen.

It was very exciting, except for the fact that, in the months prior to leaving, I had fallen head over heels for one of my childhood friends. It was very intense, my first big love. Oh, dear! I have been told that there were bucket-loads of tears at the airport the day we left. The two of us were devastated. We clung to each other desperately, but had to say goodbye. I boarded my first ever flight, en route to a new life in Australia.

Australia was known as the lucky country and the next nine years of my life would be part of a new beginning. I successfully finished my last year of high school. It was a totally new world for me; I had to make new friends again, study in a new environment, study in a new country with different school systems. I had a lot to take in that first year, but I managed to do it successfully.

Whilst doing my HSC (Higher School Certificate) at Pembroke High in Mooroolbark, Victoria, we had some career advice. It was always my wish to go to university and study languages. The teacher in charge of giving this advice, told me that I wouldn't be able to study languages at a university level, because I didn't study any foreign languages as subjects in high school. That was a very big disappointment for me.

When I finished HSC, I was offered a place at La Trobe University. I wasn't too sure what to enrol in. I decided on social work. Some of the subjects included were Politics, Sociology and English.

I wasn't doing what I really wanted to do. I was extremely unhappy and the subjects that I chose were only chosen on the spur of the moment. I didn't exactly know what I had gotten myself into. I didn't think at the time to seek advice on campus. If I had, I would have heard a different story and my life may have turned out differently.

After an entire first year of studying subjects that I immensely had little to no interest in, I decided that I didn't want to continue. I deferred and went off to find a job. This was probably not the best thing to do; once I started earning money I lost sight of my vision.

Note to Self: *Don't always accept what you're told. Do your due diligence.*

My first job was in administration, in the government sector. I made some really good friends, who are still in my life today. That is at least one good thing to come out of that job. I made the best out of the situation, having fun whilst at work. We used to play jokes on each other and tried to outdo each other. When I got undressed for bed, I would find loads of paper clips in my clothes. These came from colleagues who walked past me in the office and threw them down my top or the back of my jacket. There was lots and lots of laughing.

When I was nineteen, a friend of mine decided to go to Europe and asked if I wanted to join her. We started planning and saving for it. Unfortunately, shortly before we were meant to leave, she pulled out because she'd met someone who didn't want her to go. I decided I would go on the trip anyway. I was going to connect with my childhood love, who happened to be in Europe at the same time.

I spent six weeks in Europe, visiting a pen pal in Germany and travelling to London, France and Netherlands. I never got to connect with my childhood love. Instead, I ended up meeting my husband-to-be in Germany. He was good friends with my pen pal, having gone to school together. At the time, I was mildly intrigued by his persona and his looks. I deemed him a touch arrogant when we were introduced (a trait I grew to detest later on).

A bit of holiday romance set in when we were together. I was speechless when he asked me to marry him on the eve of my return Down Under. We had only known each other for a couple of weeks. I had no hesitation in declining his cheeky proposal. I even told him he was crazy to ask after knowing me merely a short time – we had probably spent less than one day together in total if I calculated the hours spent.

Upon my return, I decided to do a little bit of a career change by going into the police academy to become a police officer. It was fun, lots of hard work and lots of physical training. I graduated and started working in the police force.

In the meantime, I stayed in touch with my European

sweetheart, and managed to develop and maintain a long-distance relationship for over four years. In the August of 1988, he asked me to marry him again. This time I felt I could say yes. We married a year later at the Police Academy Chapel in Glen Waverley.

In 1990, after leaving the police force, I set off for another new life with my hubby in Europe. It was an exciting new adventure at the time, especially since it had been one of my dreams to live overseas. As a child, my dream was to study languages, become an air hostess and travel the world whilst working and living overseas. So in a way, by moving to Germany, one of those dreams had actually come true!

Another reason why I decided to go over there was because he was still studying. It was then up to me. I had also opened myself up to the possibility of leaving my job, my family, and my friends. It wasn't a question for me at the time to go over there and settle in his home.

In hindsight, I wonder why we had to go there and why he couldn't study in Australia, considering I already had an established career. Never mind, it wasn't meant to be. When we arrived in Germany, I, with my minimum local language skills, took on the culture and maintained two jobs to support our lifestyle. This allowed my husband to concentrate on his studies. I worked in a private enterprise, and as a teacher and tutor of English in a language school.

By moving overseas I gained a second family. My in-laws accepted and treated me as their own child, especially as there were only boys. This was good in many ways, since I didn't have my own family around me.

It wasn't long after we settled, that little negative things popped up into our relationship.

Things that were not quite okay in the way I was being treated by him. If I remember correctly, it wasn't even one or two years into the marriage that the bubble burst, the bubble of happiness, the bubble of bliss. I was accused of having an affair with a work colleague, which was totally uncalled for. No amount of denying the case helped clear this up or make him understand. I had good relationships with most of my colleagues, regardless of whether they were male or female.

I would come home after work and share with him some daily experiences from the office. Usually, I received some negative comment about anything I shared. After a while, I kept things to myself to avoid this negativity. This ultimately scarred our level of communication (something that is so important in a relationship). Slowly, I became unhappy. I wasn't able to talk about things, whether they were good or bad. I couldn't let off steam or laugh about things.

After a year or two living in Germany, my parents came to visit us for an extended period of time. On the very day they arrived, my mum said, 'You're not the same. You don't seem your usual happy self.' And that made me think. I realised my mum was right – I hadn't been smiling as often as I once did, or laughing as much as I used to. I was different. I had changed. And I wondered why.

Yes, there had been those little instances that had caused me to change my demeanour. He behaved in a volatile manner on several occasions and kept a tight rein on our finances. At the time, I regarded it as good saving habits. In hindsight, I know now this was way too restrictive and not the norm. When I wanted to study further to advance my career prospects, I was told that it would be too expensive. I accepted this to keep the peace. We were not financially uncomfortable, as we hadn't started a family yet, so pursuing studies would have been manageable.

Not long after that, a few days before Christmas, we had a really big row between the two of us. I really can't remember what it was about anymore, it was so long ago. He pushed me up against the wall, grabbed the top of my shirt and held my throat. My parents witnessed this violent action. I haven't shared this with anyone before, but I feel that I need to share this now. It is something that I should *not* have allowed.

Shortly afterwards, my husband demanded, in a not-to-be-misunderstood way, that my parents and I leave the flat we lived in. Like an obedient dog, I allowed him to put us out the door. Not just me, but also *my parents*. It was the middle of a harsh winter, and we had nowhere to go. The only place I could think of to go to was my in-law's.

I didn't know where else to go; I had no close friends to turn to as I hadn't been in the country long. The only friends I had were *his* friends from long before I came onto the scene. I didn't feel that I could go to them for help. Luckily, we didn't have that far to walk in the snow to their house. I was like a dog let loose onto the streets with my parents in tow, our tails between our legs. I was disgusted and at a loss for words.

We rocked up at his parents, who wholeheartedly let us in. I explained to them what had happened, but I cannot recall how they reacted. My German was not as good as it is now, so I wouldn't have been able to convey the event properly. I don't remember how long we stayed there or what they said to him when he came over. I just know that it was a horrible situation to be in, even more so because my parents were involved. That was the year Christmas lost the magic it used to have. It had faded within the space of minutes.

It was a big blow to the trust that I felt towards my husband, the person who I thought I loved very much, the person who had declared his undying love to me.

I started to make excuses for him and for myself:

'Maybe he was a bit stressed out because of the exams.'

'Maybe it was my fault.'

'Maybe I shouldn't have said that.'

'Maybe I shouldn't have done that.'

'Maybe it was because of the situation we were in.'

Maybe, maybe, maybe ...

I felt ashamed. I felt vulnerable, sad, and unhappy. My shame was also for my parents, that something like this could happen to them. For a long time I was very, very embarrassed. I couldn't look my parents in the eye. I felt that this person, who I'd trusted and loved, could do that to *my* parents – his parents-in-law. He should have been looking up to them and respecting them as his own.

It caused a lot of unhappiness and unease. We pretended that, after a while, it was okay. And it wasn't. I think they wanted to return home, but stayed on in misery, pretending to enjoy Christmas for my sake. When they left, things returned to normal – or as normal as you can imagine.

I continued working and life just went on. Five years later, our first daughter, lovely Laura, was born. Everything seemed to be in order; she was absolutely beautiful – and still is! I was able to nurture her and to look after her, while still teaching part-time. When she was around two, things were sometimes okay, sometimes not. I have put a lot of things into the back of my memories. There are a lot of things I can't remember anymore. Sometimes people remind me of these memories. It's almost as if I don't want to have them. I think there are a lot of things that I choose to wipe out of my mind.

When Laura was a couple of years old, something happened in my life that not many people know about. I don't often speak of it, because I have learnt to forgive myself. It happened without me forcing it, and it happened at a time when I was very vulnerable. I fell for someone. I didn't understand how I could do that. It was one of the worst things I ever imagined happening to me as a married woman! I remember conversations with friends, talking about how we couldn't comprehend people going astray in their marriage, or how they could end up with someone else. And, then it happened to me. I was devastated I allowed it to happen.

It was a very short fling and it was so intense, I was actually prepared to leave my marriage. What I got from this other person was a lot more meaningful to me than what I was getting from my own husband. That's the best way I can put it for now. When it happened, a friend of mine said, 'It wouldn't have happened if your marriage was intact.' Wow, true words, I felt.

However, that was a very small consolation. I hated myself for doing something I had always condemned other people for. How could I hurt my husband in that way? When I confessed to him about it, it was the worst thing that could have happened to him. I could see how he crumbled. I wasn't thinking of how he'd treated me in the past. I was only thinking of the hurt I had caused him. My first reaction was to leave. After some backwards and forwards, he begged me to stay. I chose to stay and make a go of our marriage again. Whether that was the right thing to do, I don't know. I know that I stayed because I wanted to make amends. I had hurt him and I had disappointed him by falling in love with someone else.

We decided that we'd go to Australia. One could say that this was running away from the problem. Looking back, I don't think it solved anything, it merely put a bandage on it. We didn't discuss the reasons why I had fallen for someone, or how we could move forward. We also didn't discuss much about forgiveness.

The year we went to Australia, was the worst year of my marriage. Things were at rock bottom. It would've been easier to just leave, to separate, but that was not the journey we were meant to be on.

Note to Self: *Always talk about the issue at hand, to process it – if you can't talk to each other, you have a problem.*

Towards the end of that year, my husband decided that he wasn't really happy in Australia. Things weren't going as well as we had hoped. He wanted to go back home. He was prepared to do it with or without me and Laura. Something inside me decided that I should pack up and go with him again. So, after twelve months of being in Australia, we left the country. With this decision, I had again committed – fully committed – to doing what was right for the marriage and our relationship.

We went back to Europe, where I worked in three jobs. Before we had even left Australia, I'd organised to go back to my old teaching job again and then I found two more when we were there. For one job, I had 7.00am starts. That lasted for a few months, until I realised Laura wasn't coping well with this arrangement. She had trouble getting up in the morning to leave, and then being left at the kindergarten. It was a very stressful time for all of us. I started wondering whether it was really worth the effort and the stress of upholding three jobs and running a family. She was the catalyst for me giving up that particular job.

Things got better and a lot easier after that. I was using public transport to get to two jobs, whilst the family car was being used by my husband to get to his work. Could it have been easier if it was the other way around?

Note to Self: *Stop letting others take advantage of you.*

Just before the turn of the century, we decided to have another baby. Or maybe I decided to let it happen, because I knew we both wanted to add to our family. I had a few pregnancy issues, including a bad back. At times, I had difficulty moving around and getting out of bed was with general discomfort. According to the doctors, I needed some external help with the housework, cooking and such. It was obvious that I was unable to take care of the house as well as the family. I felt that I wasn't getting much support from my husband in this regard, despite asking him for help. This resulted in quite a few issues between the two of us.

At one point, I decided to take matters into my own hands by hiring someone to come and clean the house for me once a week. This was for the hard tasks like cleaning floors and bathrooms. I managed to hide this fact from my husband for several weeks until he came home one day while the cleaning lady was there. Sprung, yet again! It is an understatement to say that he was very angry about this, especially about paying someone to do the housework.

I managed to get his back up yet again when I took his shirts to the local drycleaners to have them ironed. I was told in a very demeaning manner that he would not pay anybody to iron his shirts. This made me feel loved, indeed, considering I'd been ironing his shirts and doing the housecleaning for free! Maybe my hourly rate was too low ... Whilst my body was becoming pear-shaped, our relationship was going the same way.

Baby number two, little Emily, graced us with her presence as our wee bonny millennium baby. How wrong I was thinking that maybe, just maybe, things were going alright again.

I decided to further my studies in language teaching. There was an opportunity of combining that with a new business venture, where I could run my own language school franchise, teaching children English. That would have been very convenient for me, as it was something I could do around our children from home or the village we lived in. I was excited about this opportunity, although we had big disagreements around my need for wanting to have a job/career. I often heard that it was enough for him to have a career and absolutely no necessity for me to strive for one of my own. I remember discussing and agreeing that I would invest in this course of studies, yet when enrolled and I completed the course, it was scorned upon. Did I overstep the line in my need for self-fulfilment?

As much as I love my children, I couldn't see myself being a mother and a housewife *all* the time. I wanted to have some me-time, some independence, and come back to my home and children satisfied that I have tended to *me* as well, and not just my family. Of course, I also wanted to support the family and to take the pressure off my husband of being the only breadwinner.

This would have allowed us even more freedom than what we already had. Thinking back now, I was rebelling against being stuck at home. And this rebelling came up on a regular basis due to the resistance of support in what I needed to do for myself. Was this the cause of all these issues? So, I was back blaming myself for any argument that came up and any of the abuse that was going on.

After Emily was born, we decided not to have any more children. I made the decision that, when Emily was a little bit older, I would concentrate more on my self-development and my career.

Just two years later, I discovered that I was pregnant with our third child. As much as it is a blessing now, this totally threw me. I wasn't very happy. Now, I would have to put all my grandiose plans on hold again. I was distraught for a very long time. I didn't want to go through that baby phase again, those sleepless nights, the feedings, and everything else that comes along.

It took me a while to become used to the idea – almost the whole of my pregnancy. But as soon as baby Tim was born in 2003, I totally embraced him. We had a son, and I forgot all about my distress and my initial unhappiness. There was a lesson in that for me also – I needed to have Tim and I had someone who needed me.

It was around this time that, through a friend, I discovered different modalities of spirituality (apart from the religious aspect, like going to church). I studied and practiced Reiki – a holistic energy healing modality of body, soul and spirit. This was a new phase in my life and I started questioning a lot of things, becoming aware of certain powers out there, and the feeling that there was something else, something more: the driving force behind this world, this earth and the energies around us. In other words – something much bigger and more powerful than us.

I've always had these questions in my mind: what is my purpose? Why am I here? Why was I born? Why are we all on this earth? I became a Reiki practitioner and therapist. Practicing it kept me strong.

Alas, I should not have been surprised that all this esoteric stuff was seen as some 'airy fairy' thing by my husband. Whatever I seemed to find interesting or worthwhile, was usually met with disapproval. I would have to constantly justify the time, effort and money spent. Despite this conflict, I continued practicing Reiki and learning about spirituality. I even studied Astrology for a couple of years, something I really enjoyed.

I still had my freelance language teaching and translating job. I didn't end up getting a regional franchise, as my husband was against the idea. I managed to work around my children. While I taught classes, Emily and Tim stayed with me. Sometimes their dad would come home earlier to look after them (something he maintained later was an extremely big sacrifice on his part).

There was always that struggle in our partnership that kept me from developing my business further. I know if I had persisted, knowing that it would be successful, I could have made a huge shift in my income and a shift in my independence. But the decision I made at the time was to be held back, keeping myself held back. Doing what I was doing, looking after my family, playing mum and housewife, and having my safe little business on the side, I had started becoming resentful. Life wasn't going the way I wanted. I was always just waiting for something to happen to my husband's career. There was an uncertainty if he was going to be relocated with his job to another country.

For me, it always seemed to be about waiting in the sidelines, waiting in the wings, not knowing what was happening, not being able to grow my business to a point where we could be comfortable, where I could be contributing towards the family finances. I felt like I was putting a strain on it all. Even though the possibility was there for him to advance his career – despite his unhappiness with his job and the location

– I was always just waiting for him to find out where he was going, where *we* were going. I became more and more dissatisfied.

After a while, I suggested to him that we go back to Australia. He could find a job there or add to his qualifications and I would support the family in the meantime. Emily had started school and I thought that it would be good for us to move there in time for her to start her schooling.

I was hoping that the move to Australia would improve our relationship, and improve the outlook for him on his life or job. He was becoming increasingly dissatisfied with his job and things in general.

Note to Self: *Don't try and change yourself for others or change another's situation; only they can do that. It's up to you to improve your own outlook; it's your responsibility, no one else's. Having said that, it does become challenging when you're in a partnership where both parties are pulling in opposite directions. That makes it so much harder. I had developed in a different direction and we weren't seeing eye to eye on things. We weren't meeting in the middle, which would be ideal in a relationship.*

So, another new beginning dawned in 2005. I put my foot down and virtually said that I'd had enough. I felt that I had been watching and waiting in the sidelines for too long and nothing was happening. Although he wasn't very happy with the decision I was pushing for, he agreed in the end. I would take the children to Australia where Emily would start school and Laura would continue her schooling. Tim was not of school age yet. My husband didn't want to leave his job without having secured a new one in Australia. He decided to stay in Germany and then follow us later.

The kids and I stayed with family, and I was happy that I had stuck to my decision. I wanted to give my children the opportunity to grow up here, rather than just in Germany, to experience a different culture and outlook on life – to see both sides of the coin.

It was quite amazing to see the change in the children and how they had coped with that change. When we were living overseas, we were about 600 kilometres from our nearest family members. In Australia, we were with family again. That made a big difference and the kids flourished. Laura and Emily even flourished in the different school system.

We seemed to be doing okay in the first couple of months. Fortunately, my husband agreed to send some money. This made things easier for myself and the children until he could join us. This was also something he complained about profusely during those months, as well as the years that followed. After about seven or eight months, my husband joined us in Australia.

Everything was fine for a little while and then the abuse started again. It had escalated this time and had become more regular. It was a mixture of verbal, emotional, mental and psychological.

Due to work issues in Germany, he came to Australia without a job. I think he was quite dissatisfied about this and may have felt powerless. He had a very strong will and was always the decision maker. I, to keep the peace, allowed him to make decisions or I'd just step back, best not be responsible for the outcome. Even if I was in agreement with a decision, I always allowed him to make it. Regardless, he needed to find work.

I was also struggling to find a job during this time. I wanted to have a part-time job, as Tim was still little.

For whatever reason, I could not find anything. I felt I didn't want to teach anymore after doing it for so long. I'd had quite a big break between full-time work and part-time work since having babies. I wasn't able to show adequate work experience. Perhaps these contributed to the struggle of finding a position.

I considered going back to studying or starting a new business of some sort. I even considered going back to my old position in the police force. My husband didn't want me to rejoin the police force. It was just another thing met with his disapproval. I still wasn't able to get anything, despite studying a few different courses since returning to Australia.

I decided to start up a network marketing business. I struggled to find and keep customers, and I struggled getting the business off to a great start. I couldn't understand why this was happening. I know now: deep down, I needed to look after myself first.

There were a lot issues going on internally as well as externally. Part of this included my low self-esteem. There was absolutely nothing wrong with the business model, it was just me. At the time, I didn't realise the abuse became more regular. I was unhappy and I think he was unhappy too. It seemed to me like our lives were just a downward spiral and it was happening really, really fast. There seemed to be no control. Even when he managed to find a well-paying job, it was still unsatisfactory.

We'd bought a house in the meantime. Our very first house. We'd been married for so long and I thought maybe buying a home would be good for us as a couple and a family. Soon, this didn't seem to make a difference at all.

I was happily pretending to my family, my friends and my children, that everything was fine, life was just peachy. I kept the family going on the surface and I looked after the house as best as I could. I made sure the kids were fed, they were taken to school and that they had their different activities.

Things just kept getting worse and worse. Our financial situation was no good and the different businesses I had gone into had made things worse. I was blaming myself and my husband was blaming me. I was trying to make things better and looked like I was failing miserably.

At the same time, the abuse escalated further. Little did I know that what was going on had a name – 'domestic violence'. I didn't want to put myself into a position of accepting this or acknowledging I was actually going through it. One day, a friend told me that I should look at this particular website. I went onto this website late one night, when I was so miserable and not knowing which way to turn. On the first page, I read: 'If you have experienced or are experiencing any of these things, there's a possibility that you are going through domestic violence or that you're the victim of domestic violence.' I could tick almost all of the boxes.

I was amazed that there were so many types of abuse – verbal, emotional, psychological, social, physical, sexual and financial. Then there were other symptoms and behaviours an abuser demonstrates – intimidation, causing fear, controlling behaviour, homicide, preventing the abused from practicing their spirituality, and the pain of separation after the end of the relationship. (If you would like to find out more about the symptoms or signs of these types of abuse, check out the list of resources provided.)

That moment was a big eye opener for me. As I sat there, hand covering my mouth, staring at the computer screen, I thought, 'Oh, my gosh! How could I *not* see it? How could I *not* see this happening to me? And how could I *allow* it? How could I *accept* it? How could I *allow my children* to live in this situation?'

When the shock passed, I started taking action – or as much action as I could take at the time.

The next day, I rang a resource centre and spoke to someone about my situation. Next, we made an appointment for me to see an intake and caseworker. From here, there was counselling, as well as speaking to people about my options. I didn't feel strong enough to get out of my situation just yet.

I yearned and learned to ask for even more help, to do something against what had been happening to me and my kids. Yes, they too experienced it, both directly and indirectly. My own children witnessed many times the verbal abuse, the intimidation and the controlling behaviour my husband had over me. It's important to understand that if your children witness you being abused, that in itself is a form of abuse.

I dreaded weekends. They were laden with arguments and altercations. On one weekend in particular, things were no different. I can't recall what started this particular event. He was preventing me from taking washing out of the dryer for some reason. I followed him into the family room (the children were watching television at the time), where the ironing board was. I struggled to get the washing basket off him. He was angry and insisted on doing the ironing himself.

The struggling caused the heavy iron on the ironing board to thump to the floor. This only made matters worse, as he blamed me for letting the iron fall. The children were watching all this with interest and fear, not being able to do anything about it. I walked out of the room, wanting to escape the situation, to prevent it from escalating even further.

I headed towards the kitchen and he followed close behind me. As I turned, he pushed against me, causing me to fall heavily against the door frame. My cries of hurt and shock alarmed the children. They came running to my aid. This upset their father even further. In his opinion, I was the cause of this whole incident. The kids and I went into the family room and cowered together on the couch, each one of us understandably distressed. Their father angrily left the house for some time. When he returned, he blamed me for the fall, saying that I had pushed him to do it and it wasn't his fault. Was I really to blame?

Those were the kind of things that happened behind our closed doors ...

Another example of an incident where I could have called for external help, like the police. Yet, I didn't. With this particular incident, mind you, I decided to inform my doctor when I was there so I knew it was recorded.

I didn't find the strength immediately to leave or the timing wasn't right. I allowed the abuse to happen for another three years or so. I continued my internal struggle to maintain my dignity and to pretend – to myself and to the outside world – that everything was fine. I continued to allow this person to do these things to me and have him think it was okay. I continued this for so long, knowing that it wasn't the right thing to do on my part, but it was as if my hands were tied, as if I had to go through these valleys and the misery.

Was I a glutton for punishment? Some might say yes. However, I don't think so. I believe I had to go through this to be able to sit here and relay these incidents to women and men who are going through it as well. By doing so, I live in the hope that you will find the strength to get out.

I was advised on several occasions by my caseworker at the Domestic Violence Outreach Service, that I could apply for a domestic violence intervention order against my husband. I decided against this. I was afraid of the consequences, and I was afraid of pointing the finger at him and hurting him. I was afraid of so many different things, and I decided that I just wasn't ready. I wasn't going to do it.

Naturally, I endured more abuse. How resilient can one be? How much can one person allow another to mistreat her? I know, thinking back now, I was pretty insane for allowing it!

It took me another year or so to get to the point where I said, *'Yes, I'm going to do it!'* The hard work to a better life was ready to commence.

I had been a client of my caseworker for more than a year and they understood what I had endured. I was given the task of writing down all the abuse I experienced as far back as I could remember. Boy, did I dread this task and how on earth was I going to remember it all? I typed twelve pages on my laptop one night, and found that once I started, I couldn't type fast enough! To say I was terrified my husband could discover this document on my laptop, was an understatement.

I took these recollections to my caseworker and she filled in the application for a DV Intervention Order, asking me questions as we went along. This process took hours. The opportunity to change my life proved emotionally draining and time consuming. My caseworker took the emotional burden off me and transferred my trauma into the boxes on the application form. This form only allowed almost twenty years of abuse to fit into a few paragraphs. Her expertise was an enormous help and I felt at ease, knowing I had her support. She suggested we apply at a city Magistrates Court, as she believed from experience that the Magistrate might be more sympathetic to my case.

The date of the court hearing dawned and my caseworker accompanied me to the Magistrates Court in the city of Melbourne. It was winter school holidays and my children and I had spent the previous night with my parents, under the premise that it was a holiday break for us. I did not tell a soul what I was about to do. I was afraid that my family would try to stop me from making him angry at my latest decision. I did not tell my friends either, who knew so much more than my family, as they had spent countless hours listening to me and watched tears stream down my face. How could I tell my beloved children that I was about to apply to have their father removed from their lives so they could live a peaceful, violent-free life?

The moment I walked into the Magistrates Court was surreal. I thought, 'How ironic that the last time I set foot into this building was as a member of the Victoria Police Force, acting for the Crown. How the tables have turned; now that *I'm* the broken civilian, who's about to step into the witness box as an applicant.'

I breathed a sigh of relief when I met up with my caseworker at our agreed meeting point. She knew exactly what to do, where to go, what to say, and how to make me feel calm (on the surface!). I was called into a meeting with the court registrar, who interviewed me about my application. The registrar wanted to hear my story in person and explained to me what the procedure of the morning at court was to be.

Little did I know that she was about to condense my application for an IO against my husband, with its few paragraphs of my traumatic experiences, into *one* meagre paragraph that would be presented to the Magistrate, before whom I was to appear. I recall my caseworker's relieved comment that the Magistrate was a female, who may be more sympathetic than a male Magistrate. This observation was interesting – should they not be impartial in their role, regardless?

Patience in the judicial court is of utmost importance, no matter how stressed and distraught one is. We entered the court room, only to be faced with a group of members of the public who were there for their own matters to be heard. I felt exposed! Were these people, these strangers, going to be witnesses to me telling the judge my deepest emotions, my private life and hearing her interrogate me? How absolutely embarrassing!

The moment finally arrived when my name was called and I was instructed to enter the witness box. I walked over, well-dressed in my European winter coat and high-heeled boots, head held high with an air of confidence that was not felt on the inside. I heard myself utter the oath ' … the truth and nothing but the truth …'

The judge asked me where the other party – my husband – in this application was. I was flabbergasted and totally surprised by this and immediately glanced over at my caseworker. She met my gaze with a shrug. I stuttered uncertainly, and almost under my breath, that I didn't know he was meant to be there and I didn't want him to know that I was applying for this order.

She asked me to relay my reason for my application. I hesitated for what seemed like hours. I felt vulnerable standing in this box, feeling the stares of others on me. The judge verbally nudged me to start. I was at a loss for words. My mind was racing, my heart felt as if it was about to jump out of my body and my throat dried up. What do I say? Where do I start?

I bought myself some precious time by asking the judge to repeat the question, to explain what she meant. I opened my mouth and was immediately asked to speak up. The paragraph that the Magistrate had been presented with, had nothing to do with what I told her. It must have sounded absolutely lame!

I told her what happened in a recent altercation with my husband. As I remembered other things to tell her, she cut me short by telling me she was not going to grant me the order on that day. She also said my husband needed to be able to relay his side as well and he needed to be served with the pending application. My application would be adjourned for two weeks to give my husband time to prepare his case. The judge's words were something to the effect that I had managed to live in that situation for so many years, so another couple of weeks weren't going to make any difference. I was thrown into the lion's den.

That was it? Dismissed just like that? Sent back to my unsafe sanctuary of a home, in anticipation of the final hearing.

I mustered up what little confidence I was left with after this sentence, and couldn't get out of the court room fast enough. Outside, I burst into tears. They were tears of anger and frustration at the cheek of the judge! How *could* she know what I had endured after reading just one paragraph and listening to only a couple of sentences spoken under such stressful circumstances?

I felt empty and disappointed in the system – the system that I was once a part of professionally. At a time that I needed it most, it failed me. I travelled back to my parents and children somehow, my tail between my legs.

The day after the court hearing, my husband was served with this pending application.

We were still staying with my parents. He called them to tell them that I was taking him to court. I am not sure if I had told my parents myself in the meantime, or if they found out from him.

I had to go back home eventually and continue living in the same house for those two weeks. I couldn't move out anywhere because I had the three kids and he wasn't prepared to move. I felt really vulnerable. I couldn't tell my children, as I was afraid of having to explain the reason and afraid to expose their father's behaviour to them. Yet, they would have known his behaviour – they had experienced it and been exposed to it as well.

Two weeks later, I was back at court, with the application for a DV intervention order against the man I had married so long ago who fathered our beautiful children. Everything on this day seemed so surreal. I was just doing the motions.

I had a prosecutor working for me that day. She advised that the only way I stood a chance to get the application granted, was to remove the clause that stated my husband was to be excluded from the house. I wanted the order desperately and decided to have the clause removed.

The end result: the intervention order was granted for twelve months, and, yet, we were allowed to live under the same roof. This wasn't what I wanted! I wanted him out of the house so that our suffering, *my* suffering would stop, and to let the children settle. To let *everything* settle. We weren't the ones that did anything wrong, yet he was allowed to stay! Maybe the judge felt he didn't have anywhere to go. Regardless, it's easier for one person to find somewhere to live, compared to *four* (who were innocent) in my opinion.

When the intervention order was granted, I felt safe at first in as far as thinking I had this piece of paper to protect me. It didn't take long for me to feel unprotected. In the first couple of weeks, the situation at home seemed fine. My husband was behaving extraordinarily well.

Then it started again.

By this time I knew I might not recognise the abuse immediately, I was so used to it. I had so many years of living in an abusive situation that I didn't know when it was happening; it was so ingrained in me to be treated like that.

One day, in the time after the intervention order was granted, my husband sat across from where I was in the kitchen. He looked at me with such hatred, arms folded, and he said: 'Does anyone else hate you as much as I hate you? Is there anyone else out there that hates you as much as I hate you?'

I didn't know what to say. It was like a kick in the stomach, a kick in the groin, another blow to the head. He didn't have to touch me to cause that affect. For me, that was one of the worst things and I had to stay in the same house as this man under court order.

You might say, 'But you didn't have to stay; you could have left'. When one is in this situation of fear and helplessness, it's sometimes impossible to make a decision that's so drastic, and appears so clear. I didn't have the solution at hand at the time. There were so many things to consider ... I know in the end I managed to leave, but in the time leading up to it, I couldn't manage to do so.

The abuse continued, albeit, in a much smarter way this time – he was very subtle in his abuse, whether it be a comment or remark directed at me. He started to perk up after this. I was left behind with the kids, while he started going out at night and almost every weekend. I didn't think much of it at the time.

The financial abuse continued as well. I soon discovered there was less money going into the family bank account. It seemed my husband had been splitting his salary, with half going into our normal joint account and the rest went into some unknown account. This meant that, as a family of five, our income had drastically decreased and all expenses had to be paid from this now-lesser amount. Paying for every day expenses such as groceries and bills was a challenge. When I confronted him about this change in accounts, he said his reasoning was in case he had to move out after the court hearing.

Another example of his smarter abuse tactics involved buying our weekly groceries. On this particular occasion, there was no money for me to purchase these, so he went to the supermarket. When he returned, I discovered he had purchased the things *he* wanted to eat. This included one – yes, one! – single vegetable: a cauliflower. You may think there is nothing wrong with this, because he at least remembered a single vegetable. But you see, I'm a vegetarian. I had *one* vegetable to last me a whole week *and* it was also meant to be divided amongst the children.

At one point, I spoke to a lawyer from the organisation, Relationships Australia, regarding my husband breaking, what seemed to be, conditions of the order. When I explained what had been going on, I was told that it would be too difficult to prove that there was a breach. I could try to have the order changed to exclude him from the house or have him charged with breach of order, but that would also be difficult. So, I gave up that idea. Did I want to go through it all again? Did I want to spend $800 or more and go through the emotional trauma of uncertainty again? No, I was not up to that.

As I said, the abuse continued, but in a smarter way, from him. After about six months, towards the end of 2011, I was so miserable. I tried to get him to move out of the house but that didn't work. When he was home during the day, I would make sure not to be there. I felt uncomfortable around him and wanted to avoid being abused again, especially if the children were not home.

Just before Christmas, that last year of being 'together', something happened, yet again. I think he was upset about something one of the kids had done or not done and started going on another rampage. I told him, 'Just go. Please, just get out and stop treating us like this.' Words to that effect. He left and I was so relieved, but he came back again.

He begged me, sobbing uncontrollably on his knees, to allow him to stay. He said he had nowhere to go, and that he would leave us alone, would leave *me* alone. This all happened in the presence of at least one of our children. I felt sorry for him and I gave in. Now, thinking back, I should never have done it. But it's no use saying 'should haves' and 'shouldn't haves'. It was done.

I had made myself a prisoner in my own home. I didn't invite anybody around anymore. None of my friends came around; none of my family came around. They felt uncomfortable and claimed they could cut through the air with a knife when around him. That's how sombre the atmosphere was most of the time.

I'd moved out of the main bedroom and into the spare bedroom. This allowed him space and comfort, a walk-in robe and en suite bathroom. I slept on a pullout couch, which wasn't very comfortable, while my clothes remained in the main bedroom. I would hide in my new room, so I wouldn't have contact with him.

I made sure that dinner was cooked and the children were fed. In the beginning, I endured uncomfortable family mealtimes. Sometimes we were spared this. We'd eat, and as soon as I heard him coming in at the front door, I'd disappear upstairs to my prison room and wouldn't come out unless I had to see to the children. That was how my life had become. When he wasn't home, I felt comfortable to move around freely in the house. As the saying goes: when the cat's away, the mouse comes out to play!

Christmas 2011 was approaching and my sister asked me whether it would be okay if my husband could have lunch with us on Christmas Day. By this time, my family was aware of the intervention order and how unhappy I was. The word 'No' shot out of me with surprising vigour.

There were so many years where I'd felt unhappy in

his presence during Christmas. My feelings about this were more compelling than the fleeting thought that I should show compassion at that time of the year. It was the first year where I stood up and said I didn't want him to spend it with me or with my family. I had the courage to say no to feeling miserable on a special day, where people usually celebrate and have a good time with family, friends and loved ones. This was a very significant decision. My time of misery was coming to an end, even though I didn't know it. I was preparing myself to leave – I was getting stronger.

Christmas Day was spent without my husband.

Emotionally, it wasn't a very good time. Even though many of our Christmas days were spent like that over the past few years, I somehow knew that was going to be the last one in that manner. Although I had made this courageous decision to say no, and felt somewhat relieved that I no longer needed to pretend and could freely enjoy the day with family, I had taken a small step towards the big picture of freedom and happiness. After so many years of being shackled, this change in me and the situation happened so quickly. I needed to get used to the idea first. I hadn't the time to fully contemplate this decision and how everything was unfolding.

As much as it felt staged to me at the time, we still celebrated Christmas in our own home as well. According to the German tradition, the most significant part of Christmas is celebrated on Christmas Eve, usually in the late afternoon or early evening after Santa Claus has put the presents under the Christmas tree. My children loved this tradition and it was good to be able to uphold it while living in Australia. This was to be our last Christmas celebration together as a 'family', where the children had both parents around them.

Usually, we would then go to one of my sibling's houses on the same evening and celebrate according to tradition of my side of the family. We'd open more presents at midnight, so the kids would get presents twice. This year was to prove no exception. We went to my sibling's later on in the evening and celebrated in the Cyster family tradition – lots of presents, lots of people, noise and excitement, then stayed over to have the big traditional Christmas day lunch.

It had become a tradition that the children and I would go camping with my relatives after Christmas. During the summer of 2011, we did our usual holiday thing: either doing nothing or going away camping (just the children and I). Usually, holidays were not spent together, as their dad took hardly any time off work.

Those last few weeks that we spent in the place we called our family home for seven years, remains a bit of a blur.

We had several unhappy moments during this time. The summer break drew to a close and, as usual, there was some big blow-up at home. This happened the day before the school term started, of January 2012.

This particular incident began with the children mucking around – as children do. Emily had hurt herself, and we couldn't get to the bottom of what had happened, as she was crying hysterically. My sister and her family were visiting, witnessing all of this commotion. My husband took over the situation. He became upset and started screaming at the kids and at me. Once again, my family had to witness this behaviour in a helpless way, not knowing what to do. In the end, they left. The children and I continued to be screamed at. Emily and I cuddled and cowered together on the couch, while he towered over us, demanding we show him respect.

During these horrible years, I would often drop the kids off on the first day of school without having contact with anybody there. I would just drop them off or walk them to the school, and people would ask me, 'Are you okay? I've never seen you look like that. You look so ... What's been happening?' I'd always make up an excuse of some sort or dismiss them, saying I was fine. The truth is, I never wanted to involve them.

Now, R U OK? days have been introduced. These days are a great idea if people have the courage to speak up and ask someone, as well as having the courage to answer honestly.

I always wanted to wait for the right time, but I know now that there is never the right time; things just happen when they're meant to. Some higher power was making things happen for me. I had wanted to leave on several occasions in the past, to stop this misery, and to build a better life. I knew that there must be something better, but always felt that my hands were tied, that it was the wrong time, and I didn't want my kids to suffer too much. Now I know that there is no planned timing and things will just fall into place once the right time is there.

Our worlds were about to crash. D-Day was on 22 February 2012.

Two to three weeks into their school year, Laura had just started her final year at secondary school – a crucial time in her life. Emily had started her first year of secondary school, also a significant time in her life.

The weekend prior, my husband had decided that, for

the first time in our marriage, he wanted to go away on his own for a long weekend. No matter what, he needed to have a break, he said. Due to this, I had to organise care for the children, as I normally worked on a Saturday and he saw to them. I suspected that he wasn't going away on his own. He had hinted at certain times he had met someone, whom he wanted to be with. It felt like a big betrayal for me. Even though we were very unhappy together and the abuse continued, we were pretending for the children that everything was fine. We were still living in the same house, and I thought the least he could do was own up to seeing someone and leave, or wait until everything was finally over between us.

In hindsight, I think he was kind of living a double life: unhappy and abusive on one side, happy on the other. Was *I* living a double life too? Accepting abuse on one side and pretending to be okay on the other?

I started to think he had been having this affair for a while. Even those times he said he had work commitments interstate on the weekends, could have actually been about spending time with this other person. I felt hurt. I was there looking after our children and he was off gallivanting. He'd come home, I would cook meals for the family and he would eat them. I'd be doing the housework and his laundry, all the while he was out leading his double life. I felt sickened that I accepted this situation.

When he came home that weekend, something inside me just snapped. I suspected he had gone away for some pleasure and then came back into this life, this other pretend life. I frantically tried to lock him out. That didn't quite work – he could still open the front door with his key. It was a miserable act of desperation on my part. In that instance, I just wanted to put an end to all of this pretence.

I managed to get him out of the house shortly afterwards, under the premise of taking out the rubbish. I knew he would leave his keys inside the house. Once he was out, I quickly locked the door. All of this was happening while the kids were home, but I simply had to act. I refused to let him back inside. I gave him his car key and wallet by quickly opening the door.

He left but not for good.

He'd gone to stay with one of my family members, which I found quite strange considering – if my assumptions were correct – he had another place to go to, or other people/friends he could stay with. Instead, he had to count on my family.

Next morning, he demanded to come back into the house, saying that he would call the police if I didn't let him in. All of this was happening while I was getting the children ready for school, trying to be as normal as possible. I didn't want to have the added hassle of the police coming around while the kids were there, so I decided to let him in. Again, I didn't want to make a scene. He got ready for work and left again (not without some verbal altercation between us). I took the children off to school.

After I dropped the children off, I didn't want to go back there. I knew I couldn't stay another night in that house. I was very distraught and a complete wreck. I was afraid he had come back in the meantime and I didn't want to be in his presence, so I drove to a friend's place.

She knew that things had been wrong for a long time. Unfortunately, she had witnessed my husband's behaviour on occasion, and saw the impact this had on myself and the children. I managed to somehow speak up about what had occurred in the previous twenty-four hours. She said: 'You know, if you want to move out, you can always come and stay here.' She offered me a lifeline. The moment had arrived, the timing was right. I grabbed this lifeline. I had made my decision!

Something had taken over me. I knew, deep down, I did not want to go back. I knew that I had to leave my miserable life, my relationship and my home behind, and stay with my girlfriend, but I didn't quite know how I was going to do it in that moment. I didn't know where I was going to get my strength from. I didn't know how I was going to start over again. I knew the 'what' of finally ending my misery, but I didn't know the 'how'.

I felt so helpless. I felt like a child in a foreign country who didn't know the language. My friend had to spell it out for me: 'You go back home, pack your clothes, pack the kids' things, and you pack whatever else you need that you don't want to leave behind.' It wasn't her decision, but she was holding the space for me to decide. She was holding the space for me to say yes or no.

Laura was meant to finish earlier that day at 11.00am and I was originally going to pick her up from school. Instead, I called her to say that she should go to my friend's, wait there for me, and I would explain what was going on.

In the meantime, I drove back home. When I got there, I still didn't know what to do. I went inside and I walked aimlessly in and out of each room. It hit me that this could possibly be the last day I stood in this house. I also knew I had to get out on that particular day, and that if I didn't, I would never be able to leave.

I felt sick in the pit of my stomach when I thought of staying another day, let alone another year, for Laura to finish her last year at school. I could not even bear to think of it. I picked up the phone and I called my friend again. She instructed me on what to do, ran it by me once more: 'You pack your clothes, you pack the kids' things, and you pack whatever else you need that you don't want to leave behind.'

I started doing everything as quickly as I emotionally could. I wanted to be out of there before my children finished school. Thank goodness my husband didn't come home during this time.

After dropping off the first lot in my small car to my friend's place, I took Laura with me next. I explained to her what was going on, telling her that I couldn't go back there anymore. Because of her age, I had to give her the choice of coming with me or staying in the house with her dad. This was one of the hardest things that I've ever had to do.

She decided to leave with me. We went back home together and she packed her things, while I packed what I thought we would need. We took personal belongings and paperwork, my work things, and the computer – I thought the children would need that. Next, I took some of the children's clothing, some of their toys, their pillows and things dear to their hearts. I couldn't take everything, though.

With the last carload, I went to pick up my son from his school. There was only space left in the car for Emily, who was coming back from a school camp. The car was packed to the brim. I needed to explain to Emily and Tim what was happening, that we were not going back home. I think it hit Emily the hardest. She had left for the camp two days earlier and came back to this. She didn't go back to that house until months later.

That marked the end of our old life and the beginning of our new life. D-day was out of my control. I had made a split-second choice, the wheels were in motion, mother duck started walking, and the ducklings followed. I didn't have to wait for them to line up.

We moved into my girlfriend's house, already filled with her own children and another friend staying there temporarily. My husband would have arrived home from work later to an ominously vacant house, empty of the usual family noises, sights and smells. He would have noticed the missing computer in the study room.

I think that's when he called to find out what was going on. I was terrified to answer the phone, so I didn't answer the first couple of times. I knew I had to speak to him eventually, so I forced myself to answer the call, and said that we weren't coming back. I can't remember his reaction at these words. Perhaps I blocked it out? I didn't tell him where we were; I didn't want him to come and create havoc.

Later that evening, I called my parents to let them know that we had left. I didn't tell them where we were either. I didn't want them involved or possibly be intimidated by him and forced to reveal our location. I just told them that we were all fine. I knew that he was going to be calling around, looking for us.

So I've left him, now what? What do I do? What's going to happen? I felt blank and numb, and lost like a little child, but I knew that I had to get things into motion. I had to act. I tried to keep things as normal as possible for my children, so there was no breakdown on my part. I didn't cry and none of my children cried – how incredible.

I got messages from family, to see if we were okay.

I called the schools to tell them what had happened and for them to keep a watchful eye on the children. I called Laura's calisthenics club too, as she had training that first night out of the house. I wanted the coaches to be aware of what had happened in case my husband turned up during training and caused a scene. Luckily, nothing happened. It would have been more than I could have handled. Everyone was so helpful – they watched out for us.

The next morning, I faced even more logistics. I discovered he'd gone to the house of one of my sister's, looking for us and told her he was going to the police to report that I had abducted our children. I thought I'd better cover myself and went to the police station. I told them where I was and that we were fine.

I explained to them that domestic violence was involved and I had moved out. I was told that I didn't need to tell him where we were, only that the children were safe. I called my lawyer to initiate legal issues, such as custody and property settlement.

I think he'd somehow discovered where we were by ringing around and figuring it out. I also think through clever questioning, he got answers through the kids after he eventually spoke to them on the phone. In hindsight, maybe I should have kept the children out of school for a bit, but I didn't. I wanted them to have that sense of normality. Either decision would have had advantages and disadvantages.

For the whole duration we never took time off to just be, to just grieve. Should I have kept them out of school for a few days, allowing them that space to grieve, to get over their shock and feel safe and nurtured under my wings? I don't know. I will never know.

Maybe it was my way of teaching them to not give in too much or too quickly to misery, and to be strong and continue on with their life, instead of falling into a heap as soon as they meet adversity? Their schools, sporting club and friends were their constants. I hope I can call myself a constant in their lives, as well. I needed to make sure these things were there for them despite what was going on.

We stayed with my girlfriend for ten days. After that, I felt we needed to move on. Most of my family members opened up their homes for us to live with them for the time being. One of my sisters, Edith, was going away, and offered for us to stay at her house. Since we had first left the family home, I never told my husband where we were, but he was very clever in discovering that we were moving on.

He always knew where we were – even before we arrived there. He was always a step ahead of me. Did I feel like I was being stalked? Perhaps, yes. But that's okay, it was all good in the end. The bigger picture was forming anyway. We moved all our belongings from my friend's to Edith's.

In the meantime, another sister, June, and her husband, Charles, offered for us to live with them. I decided to take up the offer as their place was big enough to comfortably accommodate me and the kids without us getting in their way. The day we were moving from Edith's to June's house (only three minutes away), almost everything was packed and ready for all of us to leave.

The only person that wasn't ready was my Emily. She did not want to pack. It suddenly dawned on me that she was starting to crumble. I thought back to the way she'd come home from the school camp that day, almost two weeks earlier, and how it would have affected her spirit. She hadn't gone back to the family home since. She wasn't allowed the opportunity and the time to pack her own things or to come to terms with her mother's decision. And the next day she went to school and continued with her daily routine.

Had I been expecting too much of my children? Should I have been more considerate? I think I did what I felt was right at the time. I believe there is no right or wrong answer – it's the way we cope with the outcome that matters.

So, no wonder Emily was now showing signs of being tired, stressed, unhappy and being unsure of what was going to happen next in her life. She was tired of living out of suitcases and she broke down. Edith and her husband, Mark, said we could stay there for as long as we needed to. We ended up staying with them for another week.

After that, we finally settled in with June and Charles. Their home became ours for the next ten months. It was good for us, yet it was a very taxing time too – more so on my part – because I wasn't living in my own home. I wanted to make sure that my children respected their aunt and uncle's space. I was also overly concerned at the same time, stressed out, unhappy, and dealing with a lot of things to do with the split.

The most taxing things were the legal issues, dealing with my ex and driving my children around. Due to moving further away from their schools and their sports, our time on the road had increased dramatically, which added even more stress to my psyche. I became tired of making sure that we didn't do anything wrong while staying with family – it was not a problem with my sister and her husband at all, mind you.

I was also trying to find a job and organise child support payments. It was just so emotionally draining, and no one, no one could take that away from me. No one could help me and take that burden from me. I had to go through it. I'd virtually stopped eating at the same time (I'd pick at my food and not eat properly – I knew it wasn't good, but I just didn't have the appetite to eat). I didn't have any energy. I just focused on making sure that my kids were fine. It was probably one of the worst times I had ever gone through.

The realisation of our drastic situation hit me about seven months after actually leaving. I felt that it was only fair that I now had the chance to take the kids back to our family home and their father should move out. He had been living in our beautiful six-bedroom home on his own, while our kids and I were living in cramped quarters in someone else's home. I decided to move back into the house whilst he had the two youngest ones on a holiday.

I would then *literally* force him out or try to appeal to his senses at the least. I thought Laura could then spend the last few months of her schooling spread out and have some space to study. I imagined that our children would be more settled until we sorted the process out of selling the house or doing whatever needed to be done, and then afterwards, go our separate ways.

When the children and their father returned to the house, it was a nightmare! I suppose he felt threatened – I was back in the family home all of a sudden. He was still persistent he didn't want to leave.

Laura and Emily refused to go back, they didn't want to live there. 'We don't want to go back', they sobbed. 'We don't want to live there, please, Mummy. We want to stay at Aunty June's.' I was gob-smacked! My children had made the decision for me.

Towards the end of that first year, another opportunity came along. Another sister, Pearl, and her husband Derick owned a rental property, which was becoming vacant. She offered for us to stay there as long as we liked, until I'd sorted myself out and knew where I wanted to go. The idea was great!

The downside was it was further away from everyone in my family and my friends. It was in a seaside town I had never set foot in before. Due to this change in distance, I would have to take Emily and Tim out of their schools. Laura had just finished her schooling by this time.

I took up their offer. My decision to move 45-50 minutes away by car, didn't go down too well with the children's father. I also did the school change without advising him. It was a bold move and I managed to get judicial permission for it.

I didn't have anything to set up my house with – nothing whatsoever, except for our few personal belongings, the Mac and I think, my cheese slicer, ha, ha, ha! I will always humbly remember how things came to be when it was time to move into our new home. It was as if the army lined up on that day. Family and friends helped us in taking a couple of car loads to the house.

I had the kitchen furnished, with family bringing crockery and other household items they had taken out of their own cupboards. Pearl gave us a dining table she had in storage. Friends turned up with a bed for me, along with a table and chairs.

The kids had mattresses we were able to borrow off of my brother, Carl. The whole house was almost furnished. We were even given food! It was so, so humbling to know that I had that love and that support from everyone at a time I had nothing except for my children and our personal possessions.

I had created a wish list and left it on the kitchen bench of our new home, thinking that I would acquire them over time. Basic things like a can opener, an ironing board, an iron and a toaster. One day, my sister, June, and my mum were visiting and they disappeared for a while. They came back with those things on my list! I had everything, down to a washing machine, a fridge and a freezer!

Note to Self*: Remember how important family, friends and support networks are. People that I never considered as friends, turned out to be my friends. They showed how important they were in my life and how helpful they were being. Then there were the people I thought were my friends who turned out not to be in times of need. Fortunately, there weren't that many who turned away from me and for those who did – so be it. We had served the purpose to be in each other's lives for a reason and now it was time to move on.*

We now had even further to travel to Emily's calisthenics. In the space or a year, we had moved out of the area, changed schools, and relocated three or four times. Moving Emily from her sports club – one of her constants – to a new one, was something I couldn't do. Tim didn't have any regular sporting activities at the time, so he was fine as long as I was around him.

Moving away caused another can of worms to open with my still-husband. He proclaimed that he was against us moving, and what I'd done was out of this world, even though we were less than one hour away. He was also against the kids changing schools. My reasons for doing so were upheld in the court and the children were able to attend new schools. Phew, just another hurdle overcome!

In the meantime, there were still the legal issues involving the property settlement, children's matters, and so on, all of which was very, very draining. I didn't have a very willing partner in the game, I should add. My husband wasn't very accommodating with anything, and just about everything turned into an issue he had to drag on.

The kids were starting to feel more settled now that we were in our own place and they were starting to cope with the way life was. We were forming new friendships and enjoying the new environment, away from the hustle and bustle of the bigger suburbs.

As well as being near the ocean, the town of Hastings, on the Mornington Peninsula, has a good country feel to it. Every time I sit at the pier, watching the seagulls and the pelicans, the boats and people fishing, I feel good. I think it was meant to be, being here. I don't think I will stay here forever, but for now, it will do.

Today, my ex-husband is nowhere to be found – he has removed himself from his children's lives. I felt angry that I moved the kids and myself away because he wouldn't leave the house, and yet, he chose to move completely in the end. Now, I trust that I'm in the right place, where I'm supposed to be. I may not have all the answers, but it's *meant* to be like this.

I'm meant to be sitting here, looking over the water. I'm comfortable knowing, too, that my journey's not complete by any means; it's not over yet. And I know that there will be a few stumbling blocks to go over – life is meant to be dynamic, that is the one constant.

Life changes all the time, situations come and go. This too shall pass.

It's not my job to discover why my children's father has chosen not to be a part of their lives for the moment. As long as I know that *I* am okay, that my *children* are okay, that *our life* is okay, we can live in peace and harmony. That's a priority now, and knowing that I can rebuild my life the way I want it to be for us.

I know I've got love and support within me, within my children, and also around me from my family, my community and my friends. I am confident that throughout my life and my journey, I will always have that support and the knowing that everything happens for a reason. I had to go through that miserable time in my life, even though it took many, many years.

That reason for having to endure all that I endured, was to write this book, to share this with you and to share with those who may need this kind of story-telling. To relate my situation for you to be able to superimpose it onto yours, and create strategies for yourself to lead an amazing life. A life you absolutely deserve. To be a change-maker in this world. No two stories are the same, but you can transfer those issues or challenges to use the strategies and become self-empowered.

Know that no matter what happens, no matter what life dishes out for you, that you are always in control. You can say yes, you can say no; you have the choice. And, our main aim in this life is to be happy and to be at peace.

Many times, I've had things happen to me where it's so crap – oh, my gosh, so awfully terrible! – but I could still laugh. I could still go somewhere and have fun and be funny and laugh at funny, weird, stupid things. For me, that was – *is* – something that holds me together. Knowing that I could go sit with my family and friends and just laugh and be crazy.

I have faith and know that everything is fine, that everything is going to be okay and that things are going to turn around one day. For me, that's the most important thing: to have that faith and to know that there is something out there that buoys that faith for me, when it may not be so strong.

Hey, are you still with me? I know, we all love a good story, each and every one of us – it's in our human nature.

Through my story, I am offering you the notion that it's about being okay with where you are on your journey, acknowledging it, forgiving, and finding peace however dreary and crap your situation. It's about laughing and smiling, even though your heart is aching and threatening to shatter into miniscule pieces.

If me telling my story can help someone realise that they don't need to go through this, that they can be strong and step out and up, I have made a difference in the world.

Allow the following pages in *From Misery to Mastery – Journey to Freedom and Empowerment* to inspire you to never give up.

This is my gift to you.

> 'When everything goes against you and it seems you cannot hold on for a minute longer, never give up then, for that is just the time and place when the tide will turn.'
>
> **– Harriet Beecher Stowe**

Queen Unplugged

Part Two
Looking Forward

Chapter 1:

Life Lessons

'The gem cannot be polished without friction, nor man perfected without trials.'

– Confucius

I ask myself: Why am I writing this? What do I want to learn from doing this? I think of acknowledging my responsibility in this life, acknowledging what I have gone through, facing it, looking it in the eye and saying, 'It is what it is. I create my own story, my own life.'

Just the act of acknowledging makes me feel empowered. I question my purpose on this earth. What is the reason for me being here? Why was I born? Was it to go though these lessons of life so that I can help others in similar situations? Oh, to empower those reading these words, in the hope they look at their own lives and see that they, too, can cope!

If anyone is in doubt as to whether you can pull through your situation, hopefully reading my story might inspire or empower you to put some of these strategies into perspective for your own life. Being able to use coping strategies allows you to recreate a good life, or to rebuild your life after adversity. Getting your story out of your head allows healing, which lightens the load and takes it off your shoulders. You can start the process of letting go.

A lesson I have learned is that our life situation may not seem as bad on paper, compared to when it is left in our head, when we are milling over the same story. Thinking about it continuously will get you nowhere, but when you write it down, you feel so much better. Working through your lessons of life can also heal your inner child. Your inner child is that part of you or your psyche that still reacts and feels like a child. It is also known as your true self. Remember: there is always a way out, always a back door you can slip through, to turn your life around, no matter how bad it is.

When my marriage finally went up in smoke after twenty-three years of misery, battling with relationship issues, unhappiness and violence, I seriously struggled with defining the blessing in all of that. Why on earth did I stick it out for so, so long? Why didn't I go when I realised that there were problems? Why did I end up accepting the fact that I was miserable and why didn't I just leave?

As I worked on myself and became stronger, I could start to find the blessing in the fact that I endured unhappiness in my marriage for so long. I looked at my three beautiful children who came out of that marriage, beings created in times of love and passion – yes, there would have been love and passion at some stage. They are a blessing because if I had left sooner, I would not have had them.

Chapter 1: Life Lessons

Over time, I learned to deal with these lessons that I have been dealt with in my life. I immersed myself in personal development. I love books and I was always attracted to topics of personal growth. Prior to leaving the marriage, I had an interest in both fiction and self-development.

After this, my focus shifted more to the importance of self-development. I also watched positive movies – in particular, I rediscovered *The Secret*, by Rhonda Byrne (a movie about the law of attraction, and how you can attract both good and bad into your life by way of thinking and behaving). As well as reading and watching, I listened to self-help podcasts regarding positive thinking, how to change my thinking and much more.

∞ Put pen to paper

I started journaling again – I had lost touch with this practice when I was going through such a turbulent time after leaving my husband. I would write down everything that came up for me at the time, either on my laptop or in a notebook. The thoughts would be about times in my marriage and out of it.

If you struggle with writing, try free writing. Free writing is where you write whatever comes to your mind. Do not censor your words and do not worry about the order in which you write things down. The aim is to get whatever you are struggling with in your mind, heart and psyche out of your system onto paper.

∞ Make gratitude your best friend

Over the years, I've collected many journals. I bought myself a new pretty journal that I kept next to my bed. Each night I would write down five things that I was grateful for. At one point, I would even write down ten things that I was grateful for.

For example, today I am so grateful for:

- my children and being able to care for them
- having a bed to sleep in
- being supported and loved by my family
- having a safe and reliable car
- being able to put food on the table every day.

I found that after a while, the good things started to outshine the not so good things. I found myself thinking positively, rather than focusing on the negatives. My gratitude journal became my best friend. I looked and still look for the positive things during the day that I can include in my gratitude practice at night.

I recommend starting small. Even if you cannot think of five things in the beginning, maybe just list three you are grateful for and then build it up to five. Just take that first step. Look around you. If you have children, are you grateful for them?

Are you grateful for the air that you are breathing – otherwise you would not be alive (no matter how polluted it is!). Surely you can be grateful that you, hopefully, have food on your table? Are you grateful to be alive? Do you have a pet you feel gratitude for? Is there anything else?

You might even think that you have nothing to be grateful for, so there is no motivation; you cannot find the good in your life. Again, you might not be ready, but if you can do this process, you will turn your life around, even minutely. No matter how bad our life is, there is always, always, *always* something to be grateful for.

As I am writing this, I am sitting here, looking out the

window. The sun is shining, there are some clouds in the sky but it is beautiful and warm. I can see the trees, flowers, plants. I hear distant sounds of people, yet it is peaceful and I feel good.

Gratitude will empower you.

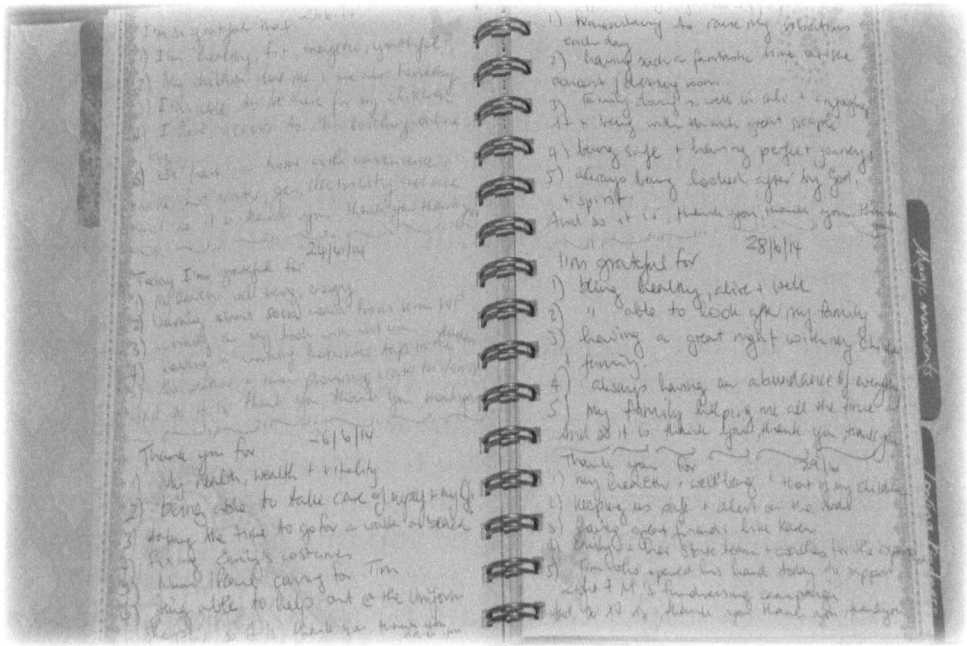

∞ Learn to forgive yourself

Forgiveness has been known to have a really strong healing effect on people, and it can change their lives dramatically. Have you heard of the ancient Hawaiian ritual, Ho'oponopono? It means to practice reconciliation and forgiveness. Ho'oponopono is about forgiving yourself and asking for forgiveness from others. It is the belief that we are all connected. All people on this planet are connected and we are here to heal the planet by forgiving ourselves first.

The ritual consists of four short and easy to remember sentences: 'I'm sorry. Please forgive me. Thank you. I love you.' That is it! It is basic and simple to implement

– I even practice it whilst having my shower! Over time, I have been able to feel the positive effect of this ritual. It creates a feeling of peace within myself and others. Try it for yourself. Repeat these four sentences to yourself, aloud or in your head (if it is too hard or strange to say out loud).

Say it to a higher power: 'Dear God/Spirit/Creator, I'm sorry. Please forgive me. Thank you. I love you.' As time goes on, you should start feeling as though you can forgive yourself, and begin to heal. You will start to look at things in different ways. When you get to the stage where you can say it out loud, great! Simple and so powerful!

If you are not good at expressing yourself or cannot say the words out loud, how about writing down the sentences? 'I am sorry, please forgive me, thank you, I love you.' I sometimes write the ritual just below my five gratitude entries. Are you worried and not ready to ask for forgiveness? Maybe you think you will never forget what happened, let alone ask for forgiveness? You are not alone. It was hard for me to face what had happened as well.

There are always two sides to a coin – both of you have innate good within yourselves, which you would have seen and loved about each other at some stage. The other person may have some issues against you as well – so asking for forgiveness of yourself is valid.

Like with the gratitude journal, start small. You may not be ready right now. If asking for forgiveness absolutely does not resonate with you right now, do it at another time. You will know when you are ready.

Only ever do things that you feel you resonate with. I was not ready to accept that I also needed to be forgiven at the beginning either.

Chapter 1: Life Lessons

> 'Acknowledging the good that you already have in your life is the foundation for all abundance.'
>
> – **Eckhart Tolle**

I focus on

∞ Self-growth ∞ Gratitude ∞ Forgiveness

My Thoughts

Life Lessons

My Thoughts

Chapter 2:

Free Fall

'The time is always right to do what is right.'

– Martin Luther King Jr.

Sometimes we need to let go of our past situations before we can move forward in our life, to make a change for the better. Letting go allows us to rest, recuperate, heal and take stock of things. Like in nature, everything has cycles. In our lives, we have our ups and downs, and, yet, everything comes full circle. When you have your downs, you have to get up again. In nature, there are the seasons – winter, spring, summer, autumn. The moon comes out at night and the sun rises in the day. The ocean has the tides. Flowers and trees bloom and die off. Animals hibernate. Life is meant to be like this for us as well.

We cannot always be on a high. When you do have low

times, use them to refresh and rest in order to move back up again. Be strong and willing to look at life differently, using different strategies and approaches. You can do this in several ways:

- Withdraw yourself a little bit. You may want to take a holiday, even just a short one.
- Take stock by reflecting on what has been happening in your life and think of the different options you have to move forward.

This time of withdrawal and reflection will start your healing process. If we do not start healing, we could eventually become physically, mentally or psychologically sick. It enables us to stop resisting those things we have been fighting in the past, the unhappiness and the traumas we experienced. You will come to be okay, knowing that you can be vulnerable.

We do not have to be strong all the time – no need to be superwoman or superman 24/7. People who are unable to let go of past situations, past hurts, can end up bitter, maybe even for the rest of their lives. Bitterness leads to unhappiness. I have yet to meet someone who actually wants to be unhappy and dissatisfied. We all want to be happy and content – *it is our basic human right.*

If you do not allow yourself to fall freely, to let go, your problems will continue. You may not be able to get rid of them or solve them. They might escalate, become worse and you may draw other problems in. It is imperative that we strive to lead a quality life on all levels. So let us look at letting go and submitting to your grief.

We not only grieve when someone passes away. Grieving can take place when you have had really traumatic things happen in your life. Things like broken relationships, losing your job or having a serious accident.

Fall into your grief, surrender to those feelings and allow yourself to feel vulnerable. Ride those emotions – remember it is different for everyone. If you feel like putting your head into the sand, do that. It is okay to be afraid.

Acknowledge it and move through it, and when you feel you cannot breathe in that sand anymore, lift your head up and find strategies to cope. Letting go of past hurts can help you move on with more confidence from those lessons learned. Let yourself fall freely and fully, with no control and no resistance, just drifting into the 'what will be, will be.'

Here are some strategies that I have implemented in my life after going through or coming out of past hurtful things:

∞ Allow yourself to trust the outcome of whatever it is that you have chosen to do

If you have left a relationship, for example, allow yourself to feel that anger. If you feel like shouting, screaming or if you feel like crying or violently sobbing, just do it – it is important to let it out.

∞ Say goodbye to blaming

Stop blaming yourself. *Stop* blaming others. Accept what has happened, and accept that you did the best you could under the circumstances. Stop feeling guilty; by healing the guilt, you are preventing repetition of the 'mistake'. You will feel strong enough to go on and lead a happier life, a more purposeful life.

∞ Learn to love yourself

Too many of us struggle with this 'I love me' bit. We never say 'I love you' to ourselves. We say it to other people – our children, partners, family and even our friends – yet we hardly ever (or never) say it to ourselves. These three powerful words will make a tremendous boost to your self-worth.

Here is a simple exercise for you to try that I have integrated into my life. I call it The Mirror Exercise: first thing every morning when you get up, look in the mirror and say, 'I love you' and really mean it. Repeat it three times.

Look deeply into your soul. It might sound a bit funny or feel a bit weird at the beginning, but if you do it on a regular basis, you will start the ball rolling and it will open up your heart. The more you do it, the better you will feel. Your self-worth will have no option but to improve.

As soon as I wake up and before I stumble off to the toilet, hair all over the place, eyes scrunched up – not a pretty sight, I can assure you – I look into the mirror, deep into my eyes, and say, 'I love you, Ruth. I love you, I love you.'

∞ Believe that the time is right

No matter when you need to leave your past, believe that it is the right time; that circumstances have led you to it, have led you to stopping whatever it is that you had been doing or experiencing.

I think back to how long I had resisted the knowledge that I needed to leave my relationship, how long it took me to make that decision to leave with my children.

'Come to the edge. We can't. We're afraid. Come to the edge. We can't. We will fall! Come to the edge. And they came. And he pushed them. And they flew.'

– Guillaume Apollinaire

I had blamed myself for what felt like an eternity, until I finally stopped wanting to be strong for others – for my children, especially. I just needed to let go. I struggled with this a lot in the beginning. At times, I felt like a rebellious child. I wanted to stomp my feet and scream, 'I don't want this anymore! I can't take it one second longer!' I wanted to hide in my bed. I wanted to give in to depression. I cried unshed tears. I screamed silently. I wanted to feel sorry for myself.

Chapter 2: Free Fall

I wanted to throw things around, but had to be so grown up all the time. I resisted all of that. I always felt that I had this responsibility, that I needed to put on a brave face to the world. Eventually, I grew tired of hiding behind this mask and let myself fall freely. I started to feel so much better giving in to all those urges – I felt immensely free.

It is okay to think and believe that whatever happens is meant to happen. When you make that acknowledgment, you will grow from it, you will become stronger, and you will become independent in *your* time, no-one else's. Remember, our journeys are all different.

Are you scared that you have done the wrong thing with your decision? Say you left your marriage or your relationship and there are children involved. Have you done the right thing by leaving? I want to tell you now that whatever you did was the right thing at the time, under the circumstances you were in. Ask yourself: what would have happened if I stayed in the situation? What could happen? What would be the outcome? Trust your answer. Weigh up those three answers and you will know. If you decide that you may have done the wrong thing by staying, or that it was wrong to leave, there is absolutely nothing wrong by admitting, 'I've made a mistake; I'll go back and I'll try to make it work again.'

In your circumstances, it will be the right choice, because you are the master of your destiny. You will know what is best for you at the time. No one else will, as no one else can make that choice for you.

Do you feel that you are not strong enough or worthy enough to step out and change your situation? Do you think you might not have the resources to do it? Know that you *are* worthy, you are your own person and you *can* believe in yourself. Have faith. Have faith that you are doing the right thing.

Perhaps you feel you cannot stop blaming the other person (that is, if you think that the other person is to blame). Learn to forgive yourself first and then you may feel you can forgive the other. Start slowly, take small steps.

I focus on

∞ Trust ∞ No blame ∞ Love ∞ Belief

My Thoughts

My Thoughts

Chapter 3:

Daily Actions

'Routine is important, I think. A good routine diverts the mind from morbid imaginings.'

– Grant Morrison

What we do each day in our lives sets the scene for not just that day, but also our future. By putting daily actions into place, we allow ourselves to feel safe within that routine. We build up our confidence, because we feel that we are in control of our lives and not someone else. By establishing a daily routine, we can plan to rebuild our lives to create a better future.

If we have set a goal, these actions usually depict the steps taken to reach that particular goal. Sometimes we have a really big goal in mind and we may think, 'Oh dear, how am I ever going to reach that?' By breaking it down we feel less overwhelmed and it becomes easy to achieve. The individual steps will help us feel more comfortable. The goal may still be a stretch but we feel more at ease. By setting yourself goals, you set yourself up for success by acting upon those individual steps to achieve that goal.

∞ Set your goal and revisit it every day

If you do not have a daily action plan, you might start to feel as if the ceiling is caving in on you, your world is falling apart and you are not in charge. We can also feel incomplete if we do not act daily on the things we want to see into fruition. Some people really thrive on those daily actions, yet it can make others freeze, if they are not seeing the results quickly enough. Nothing new will happen to improve the situations in our lives unless we plan to act.

Write your goal on a card. For example, say your goal is to lose 5 kilograms. Write the goal in the present tense, as if you have already achieved it, because it is the desired outcome. You could write: 'It is now 31 June 2015, and I have lost 5 kg. I feel healthy and terrific and people comment positively on the change in my looks.' Now write down a list of action steps you can take to achieve that goal. These could include:

- eating a healthy breakfast
- 10km walk/run everyday
- drink more water
- workout at the gym.

Highlight the times in your diary for your walk/run and gym. Even highlight your breakfast times too. If the times are highlighted, you are less likely to fill them with other activities. Stick to these actions as rigorously as you can. Place your goal card in a spot where you can easily see it daily, or keep it in your purse and look at it several times a day. I have several cards that are put strategically around places like my car's dashboard or on the wall in my shower.

Writing your goals and action steps keeps you committed and focused. You know that you are working towards something and you are not becoming stagnant. It also prevents you from getting too comfortable in your situation – it is not called 'get out of your comfort zone' for nothing ...

∞ Consistency is key

You want to work towards a specific outcome. You should always have this result at the top of your mind, with some activities to achieve it – make it habitual. It is said to take around twenty-eight days to establish a habit. Over time, it will become second nature. It is like brushing your teeth. You do it every single day, twice a day. The act of going into your bathroom, putting toothpaste on your brush and brushing your teeth is ingrained into your subconscious. You do not even think about it anymore. As I establish daily actions into my life, I feel safe and good about adhering to a routine every day. I am not anal about it, but I stick to it as much as I can.

∞ Write out your plan of the things to be done

If you are a list person, you will love creating a plan by listing the things you want to achieve. You can tick the action steps on your list off as you go. At the beginning of the week, month or even year, establish the things you want to achieve. Write down what you will do every day/week/month – and be specific. Act on it and at the end check to see if you were able to achieve all the action steps. If you have not, carry them over to the next day or week. Make sure you look at the list every day, either the night before or the morning of.

Just after I left my marriage, it was important for me that my children kept their routine going. Our routine kept us sane, whilst everything was unsure around us. I feel proud that I had built this routine for my children and me. I hope that this will instil in them a certain value that when things crumble around you, at least you keep some systems going, you establish some routines so everything is not falling apart.

Having routines also allow you to establish relationships and support teams. If things do go wrong, they are aware and can watch your back, something that proved very valuable to me in our times of need and distress.

Be aware that those actions and routines that you keep in your life can also bring forth support from family and friends, and from other people in your community, that you did not realise you had.

Not everyone will have the loving support and understanding of family and friends. There are many organisations available to provide support and information depending on what your needs are. Call a helpline, visit your local police station, community health centre or library to find out what is available. Speak to your doctor or other health care professional. If children are involved, speak to their school.

Most schools have a pastoral service or health and wellbeing coordinator who can point you in the right direction. Help is available from so many sources, so please, do not despair. Keep the faith that you will be supported. Check out my resources in the back of this book – there may be some suitable for you.

Chapter 3: Daily Actions

'You will never change your life until you change something you do daily. The secret of your success is found in your daily routine.'

– John C Maxwell

Even when my faith and emotions were at an all time low, I used to go walking. Every single day I would go out in the fresh air and shake the cobwebs in my head away. I started meditating again. In my old paradigm, I had drifted away from it. Now I felt ready to set positive routines.

Get rid of any negative patterns established in your previous life situation. If you keep doing what you have always done, nothing will ever change – you will always get the same result.

'But, Ruth,' you may be saying, 'the way I'm feeling right at this moment, with everything that's happened, I can't think straight, let alone plan my day!' Or you may be thinking, 'I don't know what to do, my mind is a blank!' Never fear; there is always a solution.

What I suggest is this: sit down somewhere quiet, where you can be alone, and take a few deep breaths. If you cannot or do not wish to be alone, do this with a friend, family member or someone you consider a support in your life. Now plan your goals. Write down the things you want to do, that will put you into that positive setting. If you are with someone, you might want to talk about your options first. Putting it onto paper will already make things clearer for you. Get out that diary, or create daily schedules on your computer – there are a myriad of templates available on the web. Choose the template that best suits you and print them. I use Google Calendar, which is easy to set up. Use it for business or private purposes and you can access it from your computer or even your phone. Working with a life or business coach can prove very valuable as well – he or she will hold you accountable every step of the way to ensure you reach your goals.

Like writing in your gratitude journal, take baby steps. There is no need to rush. Writing down your goals and action steps can seem really daunting in the beginning. I wished that I had someone to hold my hand and tell me which way to go, what to do. I yearned for someone to reassure me and guide me. I am reaching out to you now, too. I want you to feel welcome to drop me a note or call upon me if you are not sure which way to go. I am here to celebrate your wins, to cheer you

Chapter 3: Daily Actions

on and to hold the space for you to grow beyond your previous expectations. I promise you that I will assure you are helped in the appropriate manner. I am here to love and support you all the way. All I ask is that you believe in yourself!

Don't have money or resources to put any daily actions into place to reach your goals? There are lots of things that are free or low cost. Free resources are available from community services and voluntary services. For example, you can get free legal aid. There are lots of community services that will offer you free advice, and there are support groups to help you set up daily plans. You can even take part in low cost or free workshops at community centres. Fish around, go to the police station, go to your local community health centres. Go to your child's school and see if they know of any free services. Become creative, be resourceful – you can do it!

I focus on

∞ Goals ∞ Plans ∞ Consistency ∞ Daily action

My Thoughts

Chapter 3: Daily Actions

My Thoughts

Chapter 4:

Emotional Dilemmas

'To believe or not to believe, is a problem. To leave or to conceive is another problem. To ascertain and to achieve is to solve the problem.'

– A. Saleh

We all go through stuff in life, right? We go through ups and downs, and we often have life dishing out things left, right and centre. We all have our own lessons to learn.

Life Lessons = Learning Opportunity = Growth.

Life is dynamic and sometimes it just throws us right off our paths. We can have a really great plan and then BANG! You think, whoa, what just happened? What have I done to deserve this?

Chapter 4: Emotional Dilemmas

We might go on an emotional rollercoaster ride, where we need to deal with things, even when we do not know what is happening. From here, we are faced with negative emotions. We need to feel these emotions, breathe into them and face them. These dilemmas tend to stop us in our tracks, but we have to go through them, and really think about how we can take responsibility for our past actions. They could be actions you are not consciously aware of.

It is the result of your past thinking and acting patterns. Throwing yourself into that emotional ride will allow you to let the negative emotions you are facing out of your system. We must learn not to hold back, not to let them consume us. Those negative emotions are better out of your system than in. Whether you believe it or not, you will feel better afterwards.

It has been said that these emotions collect in our bodies. Then one day, just one more negative thing happens, like 'the straw that broke the camel's back'. If we do not address or process past issues or trauma that we have experienced, it can lead to illness. The accumulation of negativity within us causes the psychological burden to manifest physically.

In my case, it took many years and many instances to accumulate before I left my relationship. I once read about how it can take a person who is living in an abusive relationship about, on average, eight attempts, before they finally leave. I am pretty sure that it was around eight, if not more, attempts until *I* ultimately gained the courage to get up and leave. Prior to that, I was mentally ready to leave but I could not bring myself to do it – something was holding me back. I did not take the time to think about what was happening in my life. I did not process all the violence and abuse and so it would just go on. The situation would become okay for a while and then things would flare up again.

This is referred to as a cycle of violence: you go through the honeymoon phase, where everything in your relationship seems fine and then it happens again, and you go through that trauma once more. If you do not process these occurrences internally, it can add to your unhappiness, dissatisfaction and discord. In the resource section of this book, I have included a website address, which provides more information on the cycle of violence.

How can we deal with emotional dilemmas in our lives? The dictionary (as referred to on http://dictionary.reference.com), defines 'dilemma' as a difficult situation or a problem, which could surface in many different ways. Facing a dilemma could affect your mental state and lead to physiological disharmony. You can experience all kinds of emotions, like joy, sorrow or even hatred. You can feel in control at times and a loss of control during others.

Once I made my decision to leave my husband, things happened very quickly. I had to leave as quickly as I could, while still trying to think practically – making sure the kids were fine and that we had a place to stay. When reality actually set in and I had to start making some choices, there was no time for me to actually let myself go; I had to be in charge. I acted without analysing what was happening. Soon, I started to feel guilty, and asked myself: 'What have I done? Am I doing the right thing? How is it going to affect the children? What are other people going to say – my family, his family, *our* friends? What about me? Am I going to be okay as a single parent?' All those questions were milling around in my head – questions I had no answers to.

I would be part of those horrible statistics regarding domestic violence and divorce. I never wanted to be part of the divorce statistics and resisted for a long time. The truth is, people will go through different emotions, because each situation is diverse.

Letting go is a grieving process. Some people just go through the motions in the beginning and then after a while start grieving. That is when they realise what is going on and they start going through that emotional ride of trying to face their emotions.

> 'The right thing to do and the hard thing to do are usually the same.'
>
> – **Steve Maraboli**

To get out sanely on the other side of your emotional dilemma, it is imperative that you put some strategies into place:

∞ Cry until your tears dry up

If you can do this at the beginning, that is perfect. Do not force your healing if you cannot cry, it will happen in its own time. You might never cry. Regardless, do not compare yourself to others.

∞ Talk to someone about your dilemma

If it is out of your heart and your head, you will feel much better. It lightens the burden for you when someone is listening. They can be family (if you want to involve them), a friend or even an outsider.

∞ Let your loved ones be the guiding light

Sometimes we just cannot handle tough times on our own. We come to a crossroad. We are at loggerheads with which decision to make, which way to go. Especially if you have older children; make them a part of your decision, without letting them feel the burden of the responsibility.

I suffered in silence because I did not want my children to be burdened. I pretended that everything was fine. That was probably one of the worst things I could have done. Emotionally, everything just built up and kept building up.

Once you allow the floodgates to open, you will be fine. Allow your children to see your vulnerability as well – that you are human too. They will surprise you with their wisdom and you will be on the path to healing.

Look towards them for answers. About seven months

Chapter 4: Emotional Dilemmas

after leaving their father, my children told me they did not wish to return to the family home. That was the moment I finally broke down. That was the first time since leaving the marriage that I truly took stock. I was hysterical. Once I stopped crying and feeling sorry for myself, I felt this enormous pressure lift off my shoulders. I stopped trying to be strong no matter what and I felt *so* much better.

You may think that you are not very good at dealing with emotions on your own. And that is okay; some people may need more support than others. I tried to deal with things on my own and I also got help. Often, people prefer to talk to someone who can look at the situation objectively, from a different perspective and provide some ideas that you may not have thought of. There are many different services available – counsellors, psychologists, outreach services and helplines.

Counsellors and a psychologist put things into perspective for me again. I also went to a domestic violence outreach service, where I recounted my experiences and my feelings. They gave me advice and suggested practical steps I could take. Do not leave it till too late – the earlier the better. Get that help from somewhere.

The internet is another way of finding resources to help you, along with the officers at your local police station. If you do not have access to the internet, go to your local library or an internet cafe.

Are you afraid that you (and your kids) will not be safe if you seek help, or if you go public with your situation? Make that decision to get some help from organisations like the police. Confide in them, because they *can* help you. Make sure that they know what is going on. The first thing that I did was tell the police what I had done when I had left with my children. I made sure they knew where we were, and that we were safe. If you choose not to go to the police, there is also the option of going to a safe house. The police and helplines can tell you where to find them in your area. Whatever action you decide on, try to stay safe; you have the responsibility of your life and that of your children.

I focus on

∞ Healing ∞ Crying ∞ Talking

Chapter 4: Emotional Dilemmas

My Thoughts

My Thoughts

Chapter 5:

Taking Control

'Faith can move mountains.'

– Unknown

All of us, no matter who we are or where we are, have some kind of responsibility in life. As an adult, we feel we need to have responsibility to ourselves or to others. It gives us confidence that we are actually in control of the situation and not someone else. You feel empowered and you steer the course of your life. The responsibility for your actions lies only with you, allowing you to correct any negative decisions to ones that feel right for you.

Some women (and men) might be afraid of taking or being in control of their lives, especially after many years of their partner making most or all of the decisions. If we do not allow ourselves to take control or be in control, to have some sort of responsibility in life, we may fall victim to being walked all over. This can stop your personal growth, preventing you from becoming a better and stronger person. By not taking control, you might stay stuck in the past and have to deal with the same challenges over and over.

How can you take control of your life? Remember, *you* have the power! *You* are the one to decide which way to go. *You* are a strong person and *you* are worthy of taking control. You are responsible for your own life (and those of your children, if you have any). Take ownership of what has happened in the past, even though some of the things may not have been a choice that you made consciously, you allowed people to take control of you. Acknowledge it, embrace it and then move on. Mould your life into whatever way you want it to be. Empower yourself, knowing that when you make decisions, you are the one who made it and not someone else.

I remember feeling like I had lost control. In the beginning, there were lots of challenging times and moments of uncertainty. It took me a long time to decide what phone to get, which provider to go with, which internet plan to choose – simple things, but I was too afraid of making the wrong decision. I know now, it is okay if I make a mistake; I can 'unmake' it anytime and in any way I choose.

Something happened that made me realise I have always been in control of where my life is heading. I am somewhat of an anti-electronics freak. I hardly watch television or listen to the radio. I am quite strict with my kids watching TV as well, not allowing them to spend too much time in front of the box. But as kids are, they always try and sneak in some extra viewing time as soon as I leave the house. One day, I decided to

Chapter 5: Taking Control

be smart and hurriedly hid the remote control before I ducked out to go to the shops.

As Murphy's Law would have it, I could not find the remote after that. Days turned into weeks – it just disappeared into thin air! – and my memory was of no help. I was worried at first, but I knew it would turn up eventually and the kiddies finally got used to not having it – perfect! I just let it go. I was on the phone one afternoon, and while making myself a cup of tea, I reached up into the pantry. Low and behold, there was the remote control!

Yay, I had control again! I think that life is like that sometimes: it throws us off course, we feel like we have lost control. Things seem to go wrong all the time. It could be perceived as everything being a downward spiral, nothing is moving ahead and we are faced with challenge upon challenge. We talk about it never raining but pouring. When we stop for a while and take a step back, we can let the challenge go by acknowledging, accepting and embracing it. This is when we are likely to find a solution – relinquishing the control and allowing for things to unfold naturally, without forcing them. We are then able to get back on track and are good to go with a fresh outlook. In my case with the remote control, I did not worry about being unable find it. Once I let go of the control about needing desperately to find it, it found its way back to me.

After starting off on my single mum-dom, I had to manage everything. I was the one in control of my children and my life. I had to steer the course that we wanted, as well as trying to manage and micro-manage everything. I was playing both mum and dad, twenty-four hours a day. You need to strategically control or regain control of your life by delegating rather than trying to do everything yourself – that is the smart (wo)man's control. I lost that control in the past and now I believe I have found it again.

So now, I have the control to change the channel whichever way I want to go and I can stay on that channel for as long as I choose. I can now flick through different channels to see which one I like best.

We have a choice of how we deal with life, how we control it and how we get that control back. If you have gotten off track and think there is no way of getting back on, know that there is always a way.

You can make that choice of how you deal with your situation. You can really live your life by design; the choice is yours.

There are many strategies that have worked for me and also some that have not. Here are a few of the things I have done:

∞ **Write down what you do want versus what you do not want**

Take a sheet of paper and divide it into two columns. In the first column, list the things you do not have or do not like in your life right now. In the other column, write how you would like that particular thing to be or look like.

For example, in the first column you might list: 'I don't have enough time to clean my house.' In the second column, you might write: 'I delegate my housecleaning tasks to a cleaning lady once a week and I can use this time gained to spend with my children.'

∞ Take responsibility with goals

Another strategy is to set some super goals, even if you think you might not be able to manage it. Once you put it out there, it will come, so just take control of your life, take that responsibility and steer your life in the right direction.

Here is an example for you: 'It is 1 September 2015 and I have started my online business with three full-time staff members. My business easily generates a weekly income exceeding $10,000 and that is steadily increasing. I am so happy about my success and have many plans to grow my business.'

> 'Keep your face to the sunshine and you cannot see the shadow.'
>
> – Helen Keller

∞ Steer and be in control of *you*

Learn to be the driving force and how to control your reactions to outside influence. For example, when you are dealing with your ex-partner and the last thing you want is to see him. You know you have to do it for the children's sake. You must be able to handle this situation, even if you have had a pretty rotten relationship with him or her. You are the one who can decide how you wish to react.

Make a pact with yourself not to get angry or jump to conclusions. Commit to behaving in certain ways, in a controlled manner. Remember, you cannot control the behaviour of others, but you can control yours. Force yourself to do this. It will show you how much strength you really have. Fake it until you make it!

Not sure how to take control of your life and the situation? Do you feel you are not strong enough? Know that you *are* worthy and you *are* strong. You *are* capable and you *can* do all of these things mentioned here. Just tell yourself *you can do it* and commit to it!

You held the reigns before your marriage and before your relationship – before the proverbial s-h-i-t hit the fan. You can get that control back again, and know that everything is okay and you will be fine. You can overcome these feelings of unworthiness by creating affirmations – actions of support and encouragement – and taking control in little steps.

Remember these affirmations by putting them where you can see them every day. Repeat and affirm them regularly and use them before stepping into that 'negative zone'. Stop, breathe, affirm, shoulders back and away you go!

∞ Write down what steps you will take to be in control

Each time you are going to be dealing with your challenging situation, you can choose to be in control. Grab a colourful sticky note and write down what you will say and how you will react. Stick it on the back/inside of the front door. When you walk to the door and before you open it to that person, have a quick look at your note. It will remind you of what to say or how to feel and act.

Create some kind of method of how to be, before you actually go into that situation. You might want to quietly say to yourself or think: 'I am worthy. I am in control. I handle everything calmly with grace and ease.' You may just want to take a couple of deep breaths, pull yourself up straight and confidently before you say these affirmations. A smile helps too!

If you feel that you are not used to taking, having or being in control, that is okay. Many men and women go through this. Women may pass on the control or most of it, when they get married or when they go into a permanent relationship with their partner. For whatever reason you may have allowed this to happen, you can get that control back again.

Remind yourself that you are a strong person. Remind yourself that you are absolutely in control. Feel the success once you have accomplished the situation effectively. Celebrate yourself and go on to the next victory of being in control!

There is nothing wrong with getting some outside help if you think you cannot face the situation on your own. Draw on your support team and community – the people cheering you on and waiting in the sidelines to come to your aid. Do you feel like you cannot stand up to your ex's manipulation? Force yourself to face it! Stop belittling yourself! Step out of your comfort zone! You *can* do it! Do not show him or her that you are affected by them. Stand your ground, because you are in control. Be aware that you are strong enough and you will be able to stand up to them, like everything in life.

Are you ready to live your life by design?

I focus on

∞ What I want ∞ Responsibility ∞ Control

Chapter 5: Taking Control

My Thoughts

My Thoughts

Chapter 6:

Inner World

'Real change comes from within.'
— Nido Quebein

I believe that to be totally at one with ourselves in this life, we need to go deep inside ourselves, into our core, to become aware, and to become one with our inner world, our innermost being.

By becoming aware of your innermost being, you will get the answers from within. When you go through difficult times in life, you can discover your limiting beliefs, which quite often lead to results that are not quite what you want.

By looking deep within, at those limiting beliefs, we can become aware of patterns. We can replace old patterns with new ones and set a new direction into our life. Becoming aware of our emotions and knowing that we can actually control them, is very empowering.

We become calmer when we know we are dealing with things from a deep-seated feeling and awareness of ourselves, and not something that has been imposed on us by others.

Sometimes, we do not know which way to turn or what decisions to make. Yet, if we are in tune, in sync with our inner being, it is there that we find the answers we are looking for.

I once read that 95% of our journey is awareness. So let us delve into our inner world, where it is said that our soul or our spirit is embedded. This is where our memories are stored and our thoughts and desires are born, something we tend to forget as we grow up.

One often hears that children are very much themselves, they do and say things from the heart. They act from their gut feeling, their intuition. Children know when they do not like a person or a situation without being able to explain why.

Instead, they cling to or hide behind their parents. Yet, they can be drawn to a person that neither parent may like at all. These things come from an inner space of knowing.

As we grow up, we tend to lose that authenticity, and some people veer off in such different directions. For me, it was very important to become more in sync with my inner truth, my awareness.

For me, it was the journey to learn and discover the blessing in what I was, and am, going through in my life. I think, as a society, we have lost touch with that – this intuition, our sixth sense, our inner knowing.

Awareness means being vigilant and watchful. You have a knowing and feel things as they come up. You become more observant of situations and people who come into your life.

You also become a witness of yourself as well, of what is going on in your world, around you and within you.

As you become more conscious of being aware, you will start to look for answers. You will begin to understand why your outer world – your outer reality – has been looking the way it did/does, because of certain limiting beliefs.

∞ Learn to meditate and become aware of Self

I have felt the need to meditate over the years, since becoming aware of my spiritual Self. I have made it a habit in my life. When I was at my lowest, I meditated. It was then that I was able to connect with my heart.

I was able to just be quiet and become aware of thoughts and feelings that were going on within me.

When you meditate, you can observe those thoughts and feelings that come up and then just let them go. I feel blessed to have this ability.

Certain revelations may come up for you when you meditate. They may not happen in the beginning of your meditation journey. The answers may not come immediately in that session.

They may come much later or in the form of something happening or someone helping you. If you are new to meditation, keep at it – especially if you do not notice any immediate change – the benefits are not always obvious.

Just becoming still has an empowering affect. It is such a wonderful feeling to just sit quietly and just be – being in the moment of not doing anything, not thinking of anything. I love to meditate and would love to do it for hours.

More and more medical experts are recommending that people meditate to improve their health. Meditation causes our heart rate to slow down, which leads to physiological and psychological adjustments within.

Other benefits of meditation include lowering blood pressure, reduction in stress levels and improved concentration.

I have included a website in the resource section at the back of this book, where you can find out more about the health benefits of meditation.

∞ Create power affirmations or mantras

An affirmation or mantra is a positive sentence or statement that is repeated frequently.

You use them to remind yourself of how you would like to be, certain ways to behave and/or things you would like to have in your life. The shorter you keep them, the easier they will be to remember.

Repeat them regularly – especially when you are in that particular situation where you want to be in control. Affirmations are powerful and effective. They prepare you for great things to happen and for great change within you.

You can think an affirmation, read one, say one and even *feel* an affirmation. Be bold and creative when creating them. Start them with 'I am', 'I have' or 'I feel'.

Here are a few to get you going:

- I feel youthful, healthy and vibrant
- I am successful in everything I do
- I have the freedom to decide what is good and right for me.

∞ Connect with nature

By connecting with nature, you can take your mind off the turmoil during times of trouble. Right now I am sitting with bare feet tickling the grass, seeing its deep green colour all around me.

I pick a blade and smell its sweetness. It is such a wonderful feeling to be amongst the trees, hearing the chirping birds over my head.

The fresh air and warm sunshine are all an added bonus. How can I not feel the connection and energy?

When you feel like the walls are closing in on you, or that you cannot hold on much longer, get out into nature. Expand that feeling of openness and possibility. If you have access to a beach or park, spend some time there.

Hug a tree and feel the energy oozing out of it. Try it, I dare you! Take a picture and send it to me. Tell me about your experience and how it made you feel.

Be still and appreciate the natural beauty and dynamic movement of the birds and animals. I love watching animals – they have such a soothing effect on me.

Playing with a cute dog or watching children play, can help bring things into a different perspective. You start thinking maybe life is not so bad after all ... The possibilities for change are endless.

'Awareness allows us to get outside of our mind and observe it in action.'

– Dan Brule

You may feel that meditation or being in tune with your inner self is nonsensical and too 'New Age' for you. You cannot understand anything beyond the physical like brain, lungs, heart and so on.

If you have never tried meditation before or you feel it did not work for you for whatever reason, I strongly encourage you to be open to give it a go or try a different way of doing it.

You do not have to sit on the floor or be in an uncomfortable position – you can lie down or sit on a chair. I usually sit on my couch, cross-legged with a cushion under each knee. Find whatever method works best for you. You can go for a walk in nature, like a walking meditation with your eyes open.

You can even meditate just before getting out of your car! Sit in that quiet, confined space of your car and close your eyes for a few minutes.

Focus on deep breathing. You can do this before picking up your child or before you rush into the supermarket.

Deep breathing is much more beneficial than our usual shallow breathing and also fills every cell and molecule with much needed oxygen. Conscious breathing oxygenates our cells and improves our health on many levels.

Meditation allows you to be still and gets you ready to take on anything. Be creative about where and how you meditate. You can even meditate whilst you are standing in a queue at the supermarket!

When you begin meditation, start with short periods of three to five minutes, daily. See how you go and gradually build it up to ten, fifteen, thirty, even sixty minutes. If possible, choose a regular time and space to meditate.

You can even meditate in bed. Set your alarm five minutes earlier in the morning or go to bed a few minutes earlier at night. If you fall asleep, that is fine, you will still benefit.

There are many different methods of meditation:

- *Guided* or *visualisation meditations*, are when you are verbally walked through a meditation into a deep state of consciousness.

- *Zen Buddhism* (Zazen): Zen = meditation, Zazen = seated meditation. This is where you (usually) sit cross-legged with your hands in your lap, palms facing upward. You clear your mind and concentrate only on your breathing. Try it at http://www.wikihow.com/Begin-Zen-Meditation-%28Zazen%29
- Mindfulness meditation is where you focus your mind on the present moment, the here and now. With this relaxing meditation you are aware of your thoughts and feelings without judging or analysing them. An excellent resource for all ages is www.kidsmatter.edu.au.

You can meditate whilst having relaxing music in the background. Of course, you can also meditate without music in plain silence. I have tried all these mentioned here and liked all of them.

I most often meditate without music as I find it easier and I can do it anywhere without having to worry about a music device. With practice you can meditate even in a crowded, loud space! Join a meditation group in your local area or go on a meditation retreat. Experiment and discover what works best for you. You will get better and gain even more benefits.

You may say that you do not have time to connect with nature. Do you walk or go running? Do you walk your kids to school? You can integrate connecting with nature while doing these things. If you do walk or run, try these in a forest area, along the foreshore, river, beach or in a local park. You may feel secure doing it in the same area each time or try different locations to change the monotony of it.

Even if you do not want to be surrounded by nature,

Chapter 6: Inner World

force yourself to bring this concept into your world, either daily or two to three times a week. It is partly about getting out of your comfort zone. See it as an investment in your life, in your future. Let your creative juices flow and you will love the difference it makes in your world. Start off small, for just fifteen minutes and slowly build this up – it does not have to be for an hour.

Sometimes, when I think I cannot spare that hour, I go for a brisk walk. When I am writing and don't want to break the flow or need a break from sitting down, I go for a quick walk around the block. This rejuvenates me and I can concentrate again. Sometimes, I even integrate it with a quick shop on the way back – I get fresh air and exercise, plus a workout carrying the shopping bags! On your way to work, park your car a little farther away or take a bit of a detour past the park and briskly walk around it before work or just before you go home.

When my children were smaller, after I dropped them off at school, I would stop at a local playground set around a beautiful lake. I would run or walk there. Afterwards, I would meditate on a bench or in a quiet spot on the grass, leaning against a tree and listening to the water fountain. Sometimes I would practice Tai Chi; other times I would stare at the water for a few minutes, breathing deeply. It would not be for very long, maybe 30-45 minutes at the most. Afterwards, I would go off into my day. The more in tune you are with nature and the more in tune you are with your body, the better the person you will become.

Allow me to share a short guided meditation or visualisation with you here. Sit quietly somewhere you will not be disturbed.

Tip: You can download this guided meditation onto your phone or other device and listen to it at anytime. You will find the link in the resources section.

I have adapted this meditation from one of my clients, Wendy, who has kindly allowed me to share this meditation with you. It is called the Gaia Meditation.

This mediation encourages you to connect with your Higher Self and Guides. 'Higher Self' is a term used in many belief systems as your true self. It is described by world renowned Dr Deepak Chopra as, 'The Real You, the You inside of You', in his book, *The Higher Self.* 'Guides', refer to your spiritual guides. These entities provide counsel and guidance. When you become still, it is said that (and I, too, have experienced this) your guides can provide you with insights and a deeper awareness.

Here we go:

> *Make yourself comfortable where you are sitting. Take three long deep breaths in and out, and gently close your eyes. Turn to your Higher Self and any guides needed to be with you now.*
>
> *Feel yourself relaxed and your body centred, your feet resting on the ground. Imagine there are golden roots growing from your feet, and see them reaching and expanding down farther and farther into the warm, moist earth. And as you breathe in, warm liquid gold flows up from the earth through the roots of your feet, your legs, your torso, your heart centre. Feel it supporting, nurturing and sustaining you.*
>
> *Feel it rise to your neck, your head, flowing down your back, your arms and your hands. Feel love flowing from the earth into every molecule of your body, and*

know your sustenance and strength comes from her. Sit in her golden bliss for a moment. Now take three long deep breaths in and out again, and bring your awareness back to the room. Hear the sounds inside the room, and hear the sounds outside the room, and gently wriggle your toes and your fingers, and when you are ready, gently open your eyes.

Enjoy this guided visualisation on a regular basis and start feeling the difference. Let me know how you feel afterwards.

I focus on

∞ Meditation ∞ Affirmation ∞ Nature

My Thoughts

Inner World

My Thoughts

Chapter 7:

Breakthrough

'Everything is okay in the end. If it's not okay, then it's not the end.'

– **Unknown**

It takes time to heal. It is different and personal for everyone. In my own journey, I have experienced many different things that I have needed to heal. I have been able to heal some of these, while I am still working on others. Breaking through and reaching success in our life allows us to grow.

As we grow, we see the results of our efforts, remembering that it may take time to see that result. For some, it may happen very quickly. They may get over their challenges and issues more rapidly than others.

Their underlying problems may not be as deep-seated, and they may not have as many limiting beliefs (depending on their past). It can also take more effort on our part, as success does not happen instantly – we need to contribute our part in it. When success and change do occur, we are able to start feeling good about life again.

We start to feel good about ourselves, and can move on with our life to bigger and better things. Other people may need longer to process and work through their challenges.

There is no time limit and no perfect time when it comes to healing. Allowing and acknowledging that you are on your own individual journey is powerful.

Try not to get caught up in the drama when people say, 'Her husband's been gone for so many years now, why is she taking so long to move on?' or 'You've got to move on; it's no use being caught up in hatred after the end of your marriage.'

What would happen if we did not allow ourselves to heal? What if we didn't allow time to pass in order to heal? We would likely still be stuck in the past. We would not be able to move on due to all the hatred we are dealing with.

We are constantly bringing our emotions and focus back into that situation or onto the person we are in conflict with. It becomes so tiring and draining. Reliving the past is an unhealthy situation to constantly be in.

You have little or no hope of change, because you are constantly bringing up the past by thinking of it and speaking of it.

Then there's blame – blaming circumstances and the other person, or maybe even yourself. In doing so, you are not allowing yourself to break through to a better life. You cannot seem to move forward, regardless of how hard you try, because you are reliving past negative situations.

Let us look at breaking through, reaching that important discovery so that you can overcome that obstacle in your life. It is about reaching that major achievement, getting smart and gaining more knowledge.

Quite often we say, 'If only I'd known that then' or 'I'm smarter today' or 'I know now'. Breaking through means that you are choosing happiness and peace. Allow yourself that time to break through. We do not say 'time heals' for nothing, do we?

Relax, let go, live with and allow your emotions. Breathe into them and be aware that there is no instant healing. Allow yourself to experience the pain and the unpleasant feelings. Just ride the waves of pain and unpleasantness and know that it will be okay.

Face it and say, 'Oh, dear God (or whichever being you use for strength), I'm going through this really tough time at the moment. And I'm really, really afraid. I know that I need to go through this tough time in order to heal. Please give me strength to be able to hold on.'

After a while, once you have gone through that rock-bottom period, you will see that your life will steadily improve. Sure, you might reach a plateau again and then it will get better.

The pain does subside after a while. It will become more bearable. You might not forget the hurtful situation, but the hurt, grief and hatred will fade. I know this because I have been through it.

Certain smells, like the other person's scent, and sounds, like loud arguments or crying, will fade, along with certain feelings and emotions of your experiences. You will have vague memories of them but it will not affect you negatively as much.

∞ The Art of Forgiveness

This is a strategy I have used to help break through from my miserable situation. You can learn to forgive, even if it is just a little bit.

As mentioned in previous chapters, before you can forgive others you must forgive yourself first. Doing the exercises in chapters one and two regularly, will help you accomplish this.

Another exercise that you can do to assist forgiving yourself and others is similar to meditating. First, sit down in a comfortable spot. Then, take a few deep breaths to centre yourself and close your eyes.

Most people automatically close their eyes when they meditate but you may want to keep your softened gaze (relaxing your eyelids) steadily on a certain point. Experiment as there is no right or wrong.

Ask your Higher Self (or your True Self) to call in anybody that you have had dilemmas (or negative experiences) with in your life. Those people will come into your mind's eye (imagination). If you wish to call upon certain individual people by name, you can do that too.

When they are gathered around you, all you need to do is then say: 'I forgive you. Please forgive me. I wish you peace. Please wish me peace. I wish you joy and happiness. Please wish me joy and happiness. I forgive you, as you forgive me. I wish you peace, happiness, and prosperity.'

Then sit with that for about fifteen to twenty minutes.

You can come up with your own wording and find something that resonates with you. There is absolutely no right or wrong to this – whatever words you choose will be the right ones.

If you do these forgiveness rituals over a period of thirty days, you are bound to see some kind of change within you and even the people around you. It is completely individual.

The good thing about the Art of Forgiveness rituals is that you do not have to do this in person. Doing it energetically has the same benefit. When I first learned about this method, I freaked out.

I thought that I would never be able to do it in person and was so relieved when I learned that I did not need to. I started feeling good about my situation pretty much straightaway when I did this exercise.

Now, each time I have a shower, I practice what I call the 'Breathing Forgiveness' ritual.

On the slow in-breath, I say, 'I'm sorry'.

On the slow out-breath, I say, 'Please forgive me'.

In-breath: 'Thank you'.

Out-breath: 'I love you'.

I feel so empowered each time and I have done two rituals in one – meditative deep breathing (to improve my health and wellness), as well as forgiveness. You should give it a go! As usual, drop me a line and let me know how you felt doing this.

Chapter 7: Breakthrough

> 'For things to reveal themselves to us, we need to be ready to abandon our views about them.'
>
> **– Thich Nhat Hanh**

∞ **Allow yourself to succeed**

Start telling yourself that you are worthy and that you are capable of achieving success. *Know* that you are worthy of success in every area of your life. Create a space for SUCCESS.

Have faith that if you just keep your focus on success, eventually something positive *will* happen. Trust and believe that no matter how bleak it looks, eventually something will go right. What do they say? 'There is a pot of gold at the end of the rainbow' and 'every cloud has a silver lining.'

∞ Persistence pays off

Have you ever heard of the water pump metaphor? It involves those outdoor water pumps where people have to pump the water to get it out. In the beginning, there is nothing – you keep pumping until a few drops start to trickle out. If you keep pumping long enough, without giving up, eventually you will have a steady and strong gush of water coming out of the pump. Your efforts and hard work finally pay off.

However, if you stop pumping and walk away before the water comes out of the tap, the water flow will stop. If you need water again, it will take a lot of pumping until you get that stream flowing.

It is the same as life: you must keep pumping to get the result you want. If you stop putting in the effort, nothing is going to change. Avoid getting yourself into that position. Keep pumping, keep the faith, work on yourself, love yourself, learn to forgive, and you will reap the benefits.

So you have tried to forgive someone but have not been able to? All I can say is, just keep trying. Keep pumping, baby! Have faith that it will happen. On a daily basis, call that person into your mind and do your forgiveness ritual, 'I'm sorry, please forgive me.' Do what you need to and let it go. This will ultimately allow you to feel better and lighter about the situation. Strive to be happy and peaceful – it is your right and it costs absolutely *nothing*.

You might not feel up to talking with your ex or reconciling your differences. If you choose not to go down that track, that is your choice. You have to feel okay with it. You decide when you are ready, and if you are never ready that is okay too. *You* are in control.

Chapter 7: Breakthrough

You have been at this for a while now: meditating, forgiving, becoming aware of yourself, putting daily steps into action. And, yet, you still feel stuck. Have faith that the desired breakthrough will occur. As the saying goes, Rome wasn't built in a day.

I focus on

∞ Forgiveness ∞ Worthiness ∞ Persistence

My Thoughts

Breakthrough

My Thoughts

Chapter 8:

Powerful Support

'Friends and family are angels who lift us to our feet when our wings have trouble remembering how to fly.'

– Unknown

As human beings, we can all benefit from helping each other and living in supportive surroundings. We thrive on helping and getting help from one another. We feel safe, needed and wanted.

One of our basic human rights is to feel safe, supported and loved. By having that support system around you, or by creating one, you know you are not alone. We gain strength from others and others gain strength from us.

Our support system can be a single person, a group

Chapter 8: Powerful Support

or a community. Knowing that you can change your world by having that support around you is very important. You might need help for a longer period of time or just for a particular issue. We draw on other people's experiences and follow their examples in the hope that, maybe, we can gain benefit from this.

Some of these people may have already created a structured support system for you to tap into. It can make things a lot easier to cope when there is no need to reinvent the wheel, especially when you are already feeling vulnerable.

Having great support also makes you feel that you are on track to make a change for the better, knowing that you have done the right thing.

I believe that having support from others gives you better chances of success. You do not need to go through your situation or dilemma alone, and you do not need to feel as if people are not acknowledging what you are going through. Having support gives you a bit more confidence. Support also provides the opportunity to receive feedback, and to bounce your ideas and thoughts off others.

Some of you may feel that if you do not have that support structure in place, you might lose faith in some of the decisions you make or the things you want to achieve in your life. You might lose sight of your vision and changes that you endeavour to have in your life.

These might come around at a much slower pace, or they might never happen, meaning, that you remain stuck in that old paradigm.

When I first stepped out of my marriage, I was looking

for ways to stand on my own feet, but I also knew that I needed to have a powerful support system in place. Family is usually our first port of call when we seek support in times of need. Unfortunately, not everybody has family around them. You might be on your own in a particular country, which I was for a while when I lived abroad. People with no immediate family usually count on their friends. If you do not have friends, there are other ways and means of seeking support.

Remember, your local community and police, helplines, volunteer services, hospitals and your doctor are available to provide information, and help you implement a plan of action. If you work, there may be services available within that organization. Most companies have a health and wellbeing department for their staff. These resources are just as good as a starting point for getting that much needed support.

It is vital you have some kind of support around you, otherwise your health may suffer. Seek help and do not suffer in silence. So many women and men in similar situations to mine (involving domestic violence) suffer in silence.

I did the same thing by choosing not to talk about my situation at first. It took a long time before I had that courage to stand up and admit what I was enduring and that I needed some help. So, I decided to roll up my sleeves and get into the action of changing my life situation!

∞ Open up and be strong

Push yourself to ask for help if you need it. Do not worry about what other people will say. All you need is one person to help you, that one person who will listen to you and be the catalyst to set the ball rolling – for you to be safe and start your healing process.

One tip from your support person/community can assure that you are on the right track. You will always have the responsibility for your own change. Your support can only guide you; the final decision rests with you. Remember, you *are* strong and you *are* in charge. Step up and create; be the change.

∞ Get the law behind you

Get some legal help – that is what the legal system is there for. Admittedly, I did not think that they could help me in the beginning. I wanted to call the police so many times when the situation in our home was unbearable, when just another incident was upon us.

I remember threatening to call the police once while sitting on my daughter's bed. I had the phone in my hand but I didn't put the call through. I was afraid they wouldn't believe me, that my story wouldn't be good enough to warrant them coming to our aid.

How ironic, considering I am an ex-member of the police force. Perhaps I was ashamed that I was unable to stand up to this abuse, despite my policing background. I had turned into a helpless civilian.

I also worried about what the neighbours would think and about the consequences for my husband – his reputation and his anger towards me.

Thinking back, I should have sought that legal help. I had every right to do so. It would have saved us both so much heartache …

Eventually, I did go through the court system. I decided it was the right time to create a legal support structure around me by getting a domestic violence order issued. I had also received valuable support from a domestic violence resource service. They stood by my side once I was ready to go to court.

∞ Create a Plan of Support

You can create a Plan of Support yourself or ask someone to help you. Their help can be anything from physical, emotional or mental support, for yourself and for your dependents. Support agencies provided by the community are also at hand to help out.

Local community services usually have information brochures available. There are also websites where you can find information and checklists for easy and quick references.

A first port of call can be your local council office or the Department of Human Services. You can find DHS contacts on the Resource page of this book.

Counselling helped me to process my experiences, made me stronger and allowed me to look at my situation from a different angle. If you have children, there are counselling services available for them as well. Find out if their school has a psychologist or nurse who may be able to work with your child.

Keep a watchful eye on them or ask someone to help you do so. This will enable you to react with a solution before it is too late. Children may find it difficult to express themselves and the signs may not be so obvious.

A couple of alert signs may be: behavioural problems, bed-wetting, nightmares, change in academic achievements, depression, and reverting back to communicating in 'baby-talk'.

When problems arose for me and my children, I knew I had that extra external support to cope with these situations in a better way.

Chapter 8: Powerful Support

'My precious child, I love you and will never leave you ... When you saw only one set of footprints. It was then that I carried you.'

– Margaret Fishback Powers

There was one particular time that I chose not to ask for support. My son had been using the iPad, which was fairly new, and he somehow managed to crack the screen. Needless to say, I was furious when I saw it! I had regrettably deemed a cover to be an unnecessary extra expense.

Not long after that, my son came home after a weekend with his dad. Accompanying him was a new iPad cover. My reaction was blatant anger and annoyance at his father. How dare he buy things for my device and without my permission! We were no longer an item and it was not up to him to do this! Besides ... I would have bought a red one, not a white one! So I told my son not to use the cover.

Now, in hindsight, I should have graciously accepted Tim's clever thinking – bless his heart – and the help that his father offered at the time. Alas, I had too much pride and I did not want to accept help from him after all we had been through. I felt and knew that I could manage on my own. My son was really only the catalyst in this situation; he had not given it a second thought when he asked his father to buy the cover. For him, it did not matter, and I think he may have been somewhat disappointed and maybe even hurt at my childish reaction.

Sometimes, it is hard for us to swallow our pride and look at the practical or the pragmatic side of situations. We think that we can manage on our own. I should have just said thank you, allowed my son to use it and gone on from there. I am still learning and I am still going through tough moments, navigating my way around certain challenging decisions.

I am intensely grateful to have a fantastic support system in my family, as well as in my friends. I still get emotional now just thinking about how, when we moved into our new house. We had the whole place furnished by the end of the day, due to family and friends helping and donating their time and household items. I felt so humbled because I had not asked for that support, and as it turned out, I did not have to ask. It is an amazing thing to realise that support is there without even having to ask for it – how powerful! Sometimes, people will just appear when they are needed. They are our angels on earth. That is the beauty of this life.

Chapter 8: Powerful Support

If you do not have friends or family who can help, there are churches and outreach services who gladly assist. The first step is to ring them up and say that you need help. If you require legal advice but do not have the financial resources, there are free legal aid services. You might be afraid or feel unsafe if your ex lashes out, but remember that you do have legal rights. We all have a right to be safe and we all have a right to stand up to the things that are wrongly done to us. Call the police. Do not be ashamed and do not be afraid to protect yourself and your family. Pick up the phone; call for help. Do not put yourself in danger. Do not ever think that you are alone.

I focus on

∞ Support ∞ Transparency ∞ Strength

My Thoughts

Powerful Support

My Thoughts

Chapter 9:

Your Purpose

'If you can't figure out your purpose, figure out your passion. For your passion will lead you right into your purpose.'

– Bishop T.D Jakes

I believe that each and every one of us on this earth has a purpose, a reason to be here. We have a reason to live our lives, and knowing what our reason is can be beneficial in the way we find our true path to happiness. When we find true happiness, we can live our truth and not that of someone else's. To live our own truth, we need to be aligned with our core values. When we are aligned with our core values, we can live a regret-free life, because we do the things that *we* want to do. A life of purpose, in truth, inevitably leads to a life filled with peace – peace within ourselves and with the world.

Chapter 9: Your Purpose

Most people may never know or discover their purpose. It has been said that if those people – at least older adults – are aligned with their higher purpose, the risk of death is strongly reduced. I believe I read this in *The Passion Test,* by Janet Bray Attwood. What are the consequences of living or not living according to our purpose in life? There could always be some sense of dissatisfaction, something that does not sit quite right with us. We always yearn for something better, but we may not know how to change or know what this 'something better' is. We are always complaining we are unhappy, not really at peace. We just live day to day, making sure that we have food to eat, our kids are dressed, have a home to live in and place to sleep at night.

Perhaps you have a job that you dislike, but you still need to earn the money. Even though you are unhappy, you are too afraid to risk losing it. According to the annual Kelly Services Survey, nearly half of the world's employed are unhappy in their jobs. This survey is conducted worldwide by an American Recruitment Agency. Many people work in a position or in a profession that they do not truly value or love. A great job would allow their passion to be used and if not, this inevitably leads to dissatisfaction, unhappiness and even ill health.

So, how do you discover your purpose and your reason for existence? How do you identify this 'p' word and how do you live it? I reckon that half the job is already done by just identifying or determining your purpose and then living your life according to that! And that would be just so wonderful, right? Imagine that we are all living a happy, peaceful and passionate life, doing the things that *we* love to do. The world would certainly look a lot better and different! I did not always know my passion and I still sometimes wonder if I am doing the right thing.

Sometimes things have to happen first before your purpose 'shows' itself. I was always asking myself from a very young age, 'Why am I here?' And especially after having gone through this domestic violent relationship, I asked, 'Why me? Why did I have to suffer? Why did I have to go through all these things? Why not someone else? Why wasn't it Plain Jane down the road? Why wasn't it Mrs Whatchamacallit from next door?'

And after all this questioning and soul searching, I have realised that I was just writing or creating my real life story. So every time I go through crap situations, which will happen time and again, I become stronger. I am merely creating stories through my life experiences and they will help others in their lives as well.

I have endeavoured over the years to identify my purpose and live it to the best of my ability. Attwood's, *The Passion Test*, helped me identify what I really love. Your passion does not have to be something really out of this world.

These are some of the things I discovered about myself that I truly value in my life, and are the ideal way in which I want to live my life. When my life is ideal, I am:

- present, passionate and purposeful
- living a peaceful, happy and harmonious life filled with freedom, fun, love, laughter and abundance
- respected, globally well-known, and successful as a speaker, author and coach in personal development and business.

∞ Identify your Values

To establish your purpose, your first step is to identify your values. What is a value? A value is something that is extremely important to you in your life. It is a standard of behaviour, the ethics a person lives by. Values affect the way you love or would love to live your life by. There are a multitude of values. Here are some examples: achievement, affluence, peace, joy, love, family, belonging, education, faith, rest, relaxation, beauty, religion and freedom.

Just remember, whenever you feel unhappy, ask yourself this question: am I living my life according to my values? You will know the answer. Other questions you can ask yourself are: am I living according to my value of achievement, or peace, or joy, or love? Am I putting my family first? Do I belong to anybody? Do I have a sense of belonging? (If you have these as your values.) If your answer to these questions is no, chances are you are not living your life according to your values. It can also explain why you have been living an unhappy or dissatisfactory life.

American self-help author, Steve Pavlina, has come up with a list of over 400 values if you get stuck on what your values are. You can view this list by typing into Google: 'Steve Pavlina values'. I have also provided a link in the resource section of this book. Use whatever values resonate instinctively with you. If it does not resonate with you at all, it is obviously not a value of yours.

Make that list as big as you want and then narrow it down. Take the top ten or the top twenty values from that list by asking which is more important out of those values. From there, you can narrow it down to your top three to five or keep it as your top ten values.

∞ Create your value affirmations

You can use your list of values to create your affirmation. Use them in working towards achieving things in your life and results that you want to create. Remember, when you create your affirmation, it is best to make it short, simple and positive – always positive. Rather than saying, 'I am always late', try, 'I am always on time/punctual.' Instead of, 'I don't want to be poor', say, 'I enjoy living an affluent life.'

Place your affirmations onto your mirrors, windows, bathroom mirrors, at the kitchen sink, on your car dashboard, or on the sun visor of your car. Even put them on your bedside table – somewhere you can see them last thing at night before you fall asleep. The shower is a good place to have them as well. I have three lots of affirmations enclosed in plastic sheets so they stay dry as I read them while I wash. It works wonders and feels great! The more you see your affirmations, the more you are going to remember them and, eventually, they will become embedded into your psyche. I tend to write my affirmations on sticky notes or 3x5 sized cards (and now you know where I put mine!).

∞ Discover your purpose

You can also use meditation to ask your Higher Self, 'What is my purpose in life? Why am I here? What is my passion? What brings me joy?' Ask these questions with conviction and the answer will come to you. It may not present itself in that initial sitting or session, but later on. Be open to the different ways the answer could come your way. I read somewhere that your passion, or your very first idea as a child of what you wanted to be as an adult, is often what lies dearest and closest to your purpose.

Chapter 9: Your Purpose

Can we have more than one purpose? I think so. If we can come up with such a big list of values, then surely we could have more than one purpose, right?

> 'There is no greater gift you can give or receive than to honour your calling. It's why you were born. And how you become most truly alive.'
>
> **– Oprah Winfrey**

∞ Find your passion

Do you feel that you do not have a passion in life? Are you stuck for an answer when someone asks you what you are passionate about? It is as simple as asking yourself, 'What is it that I can do for hours on end without realising that time has passed?' Is it reading, running or cooking? Any of these could be your passion. Cooking is most definitely *not* my passion – I know I hate spending hours in the kitchen! But for you, it might be the thing that gets your creative juices flowing. Sticking a roast in the oven or creating a heavenly chocolate cake may have you blossoming from the inside and swelling with pride when you see everyone devouring every last crumb!

Sometimes life gets busy and you tend to forget to read your purpose statements, or your affirmations. You can lose track of time or you have deadlines. When this happens, you get out of that habit, that rhythm of meditating or affirming on a regular basis or making sure that you are aligned with your highest purpose. I find that travelling or having a different routine (like when the children are on school holidays), often gets my routine out of whack. I might not have a chance to meditate during these times. When I come home from holidays or when my schedule goes back to normal, I try to get back into that routine as soon as possible.

Do not beat yourself up if you have not been able to find your purpose or if you have not had the time to look at what your values are. Like everything else, start small and you will get better as time goes on. Take ten minutes here or twenty minutes there to make that list of values and affirmations. Switch the television off or get off Facebook. That will be the start to finding your purpose.

I focus on

∞ Purpose ∞ Values ∞ Passion ∞ Affirmations

Chapter 9: Your Purpose

My Thoughts

My Thoughts

Chapter 10:

Adjust the Sails

'A journey of a thousand miles begins with one single step.'

– Lao Tzu

Our life is not set in stone. It is dynamic, changes all the time and is definitely not boring. There are lots of decisions that we have to make, lots of situations that we have to assess and reassess. Sometimes we are cruising along nicely and then something happens. We cannot and should not expect our life to be just rigid. So, when we think that we have planned something and it does not work out, all we need to do is adjust the plan to go in a different direction.

Changing direction allows us to clarify our lives. Having a clear plan of the way you want your life to be, leaves you with the opportunity to start setting some really gorgeous goals for yourself and your family. Those goals can lead to new beginnings due to changing your outlook on your past situation/s. These allow you to go on a new and exciting adventure in your life! Without goals, plans and direction, you will just fluff around in life. Without them, there tends to be no structure, so we just go from one day to the next, living each day as it comes. A lot of people live like that. Others need that clarity and they need to know that direction, because it makes them feel good.

There was an interesting study by Harvard University in 1979, where a group of graduates were surveyed on goal setting. They wanted to find out how many of those graduates were setting goals. 84% said that they had no specific goals, 13% had goals but they did not write them down. A mere 3% had clear goals written down and plans to achieve them.

Those very same people were interviewed again ten years later. 13% of those who had goals were earning twice as much as the 84% with no goals at all. And the 3% with clearly written down goals were earning an average of ten times as much as the other 97% put together. So, you can see how important it is to be setting goals and the clarity that it provides just by writing those goals down.

∞ Imagine you are on a boat journey

Are you ready to talk about how to adjust your sails, and set your direction in life when something goes wrong? Pause for a moment and imagine you are on a boat journey. Your life journey can be compared to a voyage on a boat, adjusting it as you go along.

Let us say you are sailing off in a particular direction towards Point B. You soon realise you set the course in such a way, that the boat is not going in the right direction. So, you just adjust your sails, set your new direction and off you go. No big drama! That slight adjustment of the sails will let you see your surroundings in a different way. Setting a new direction allows you to clearly see where you want to go in your life, your destiny and your destination. Have you ever noticed how your surroundings look totally different if you choose to take a different route home, instead of the normal one?

It is the same with the goals that you have in mind. When you plan, you have a clear way to change from your previous life into a new, empowered one. I never used to write down my goals. I grew up having my goals or aspirations in my head: my earliest dreams of becoming a teacher, to study languages, become an air stewardess, having children and a beautiful house to call my own – the kind of goals that many have in their ideal world.

I learnt about goal setting as an adult. I think this is something schools should be teaching now, and yes, there is a growing trend for children to learn how to set goals, which is great. I hope that I can pass these skills on to my children, so that they are able to achieve what they want in life. I hope they also develop the skills that, when things go wrong, they can just adjust and tweak their goals.

When I was going through this terrible time in my marriage, and after I left, I made a list of the things that I wanted to have in my life. These were just whatever came into my head at the time, along with some really outrageous things as well. Some of my goals were/are: to have a successful international business, a house at the beach that is big enough to accommodate my parents, holiday homes around the world, and to go on luxury holidays 2–3 times a year. As my life experiences change, I add to these goals and I also remove some altogether. I have found that some things become less important to achieve, while others become a bigger priority. I believe these goals are connected with your values. If you set goals that are not congruent to your values then you probably will not want to achieve them, or would be unhappy or dissatisfied when you do.

∞ Set SMART goals

Let us say you would like to earn a million dollars, buy a BMW, travel the world, and own three houses. All these goals are achievable. Make your goals as big as you want! I used to write down where I was, what happened, where I am now and where I want to go.

Then I looked at the goals I wanted to set – and I set some really good ones! When I lived in Germany, one of the cars I owned was a BMW 5 Series, which I loved. At the moment, I drive a Honda Jazz. My goal is to buy a red BMW 2 Series, specifically the Active Tourer.

I write my goals according to the SMART principle – Specific, Measurable, Achievable, Realistic, Timely. Be specific by writing down *exactly* what you want. Ensure that you can measure how you will achieve that goal. Is it achievable and realistic? Put a timeframe of when you want to have that goal by. You can also incorporate 'who, what, where, when and how' into your goal.

Here is a SMART example: 'I feel excited as I'm sitting behind the steering wheel of my brand new red BMW X2, on 31st November, 2015. I am on the way back from the dealership to pick up my children from school. I proudly breathe in the smell of the leather upholstery.

Chapter 10: Adjust the Sails

I have the windows down with the music blaring and it is exhilarating. I smile as I notice the admiring gazes of other drivers in my rear-view mirror!' Ensure your goal is highly motivating and exciting, and bring your emotions into it. Write it in the present tense, and own it by using the word 'I'.

∞ Take action

Once your goal is set, move in its direction by putting action steps into place. Using our car goal example, you may want to use this Action Plan:

1. Do internet research
2. List requirements/features wanted
3. Work out finances
4. Visit a BMW car dealer
5. Go for a test drive
6. Speak to salesman.

Put timeframes on each action step. This way you will know when you want to achieve action steps 1, 2, etc., along with who/what will be involved in actioning them. And don't forget to visualise this goal daily!

If you have written down your goals, well done! If you have not, you can still do so – there is no time like now. Be aware that goals in your head can also be adjusted. On paper, they are clearer and you can always adjust or change them. We all change over time due to our experiences, so some goals may become irrelevant or unimportant later on. Other things become higher priority as we grow and go through life. Remember to smile, relax and breathe. Life is too short not to!

As my marriage spiralled downhill, I wanted to return to Australia, give my children the opportunity to experience life Down Under, be with my family, and rekindle old friendships. I longed to be with supportive and loving people again. The move finally cost me my marriage.

After leaving my marriage and stepping out, I had to look at my life again to assess my direction and adjust the sails. Would I have left my husband whilst living in Germany? Given all the things that happened, most likely, yes, I think so, but with a different outcome. The outcome will never be known, thank goodness.

> 'I can't change the direction of the wind, but I can adjust my sails to always reach my destination.'
>
> **– Jimmy Dean**

Chapter 10: Adjust the Sails

Are you still unsure about how to set goals on your own? You may feel overwhelmed with the process. It may seem easy enough when you read about it, but you may struggle when putting pen to paper.

Use the internet to help you – it is one of the greatest resources we have. I, myself, did some research about achieving my goal of owning my red BMW X2 – and I am definitely *not* an internet guru, believe you me!

I researched what the benefits and features of this model were, where and how I could arrange for a test drive. I used this in conjunction with achieving my action steps to work towards achieving this goal.

If the internet is too daunting, you can also work with a life or business coach. Coaches and mentors are there to guide and assist you, taking stock of where you are, setting goals and holding you accountable for achieving them. Once you set the foundations, you will be great. It is just a matter of taking that first step.

There are also books on the subject of goal setting, as well as courses, seminars and workshops. Even though I know how to set goals and coach clients, I still attend personal development seminars where we have to do goal-setting processes. I learn a great deal from these sessions each time I go and I always take some valuable tips away with me.

You might say that you never stick to your goals. If so, break them down; choose one or two action steps to start off with. It is all about baby steps. Realise these steps first or at least take some kind of action toward achieving them – move in the direction of your dreams and goals.

Once you see success, it will spur you on and motivate

you to continue in the direction of achieving your goals. This method may make it more achievable for you and give you a sense of confidence. The action steps are a way to break your goal down into mini goals.

A word of warning: you need to have a bit of a stretch too; make your goal incredible, almost unbelievable (you must believe that you can achieve it). You must have that big picture in mind. Do not make it too overwhelming. Those baby steps will allow you to see some achievement.

Above all, have fun with it and be grateful for what you have achieved already! Do not be too attached to the outcome. Have faith that, eventually, you will see the fruits of your efforts. In my BMW case, I am grateful for the fact that I have a safe and reliable Honda Jazz. I have fun with dreaming and visualising what it is like to drive a BMW. It is fun when I take one for a test drive, so that I can recreate those same feelings when I visualise and affirm my goal of owning one!

You might also say that you do not really know what you want. If you want to change your life, you must be determined to find out what it is you want. Question yourself and go back to your list of values if you need to get a better idea of what is important to you.

Once you have figured out what brings you joy, what you really want to do, then have another crack at setting your goals. It is never too late; it does not matter how old you are.

You will find that by just doing it step by step, you can achieve your goals. You can then go on, adjust it if you need to, and know that if you do not achieve that particular goal, you can adjust it to another one.

Chapter 10: Adjust the Sails

When I do not achieve certain goals, I sometimes think that it was probably not meant to be. Maybe it was not the right time or it would have made me unhappy. As well as being open to achieving your goals, also be open to the possibility of not achieving them. This will help you grow. Embrace obstacles no matter how hard it seems at the time.

I focus on

∞ Being ready ∞ My goals ∞ Taking action

My Thoughts

Chapter 10: Adjust the Sails

My Thoughts

Chapter 11:

Effortless Results

'Be conscious of your actions for they are the seeds from which your tomorrow blooms and blossoms.'

– The Law of Cause and Effect

Putting your mind to something that you want in life and taking regular action towards it, must eventually produce results – or at least some kind of result.

It might not be your end result, but it will lead you somewhere, hopefully towards where you want to be.

Taking that action on a regular basis will allow you to reap what you have sown down the track and that will leave you with a feeling of satisfaction.

Just knowing that your work has paid off will enable you to sit back and enjoy the result.

Chapter 11: Effortless Results

You may not consciously sit down and relax or sit back and enjoy, but you will acknowledge it. You will know when you have reached that goal when you have seen the results.

When you are successful in achieving something, you might tell someone about it, you will spread the story, you will be happy and you will perhaps show others how you achieved it.

You will inspire others to maybe take the same steps to create a positive outcome in their lives.

There are so many stories of great achievements from people who have worked hard in life, who acted on things, who put action steps into place and who created amazing results from taking those actions.

If you do not do the same, if you just sit back and allow life to pass you by without doing anything you wish to achieve, nothing will change.

When you get the same negative results repeatedly from doing things in a certain way, you might start to resent your life. This could lead to unhappiness and being disgruntled or unmotivated and disempowered.

So how do we create something effortlessly by being in constant action? If you are enjoying the effort you are putting into something, it does not feel like hard work – it becomes *effortless*. Incorporate effortless activities daily towards creating the life you want and that will lead to results.

To create results in my life I have learned to act each day towards my goal, even if that goal was to lose weight or become fitter. An action towards achieving that goal can be as small as going for a walk every day.

Eventually, you will become fitter, lose some centimetres, gain some muscle and become trimmer.

Start with the end in mind. Hold that big picture and keep your eye on it; create that action.

If you go running on a regular basis, you might say that you want to run five kilometres without feeling breathless or without collapsing.

Rather than running five kilometres straight out, build up to it slowly by running 500 metres or one kilometre.

Keep this up until you can run that five kilometres without feeling puffed.

You can visualise and affirm the goals that you want to achieve or create in life. This can be really fun, a bit like daydreaming.

Everyone can visualise, because we think in pictures. It is basically just bringing that picture into your mind, experiencing and feeling it, and imagining what it would be like to achieve it.

I used to go and have a look at beautiful show houses with my son in tow.

One day, Tim and I spent about an hour just going through different display homes with swimming pools. It was amazing looking at them through a child's eyes.

Tim was so excited, he would run through the houses and check out the kids' areas and the bedrooms.

He fell in love with certain styles and his eyes just about popped out with some of the grandiose theatre rooms.

Chapter 11: Effortless Results

'Create magic wherever you go and your life will be truly magical.'

– Ruth Cyster-Stuettgen

By learning to look at something through your child's eyes, it becomes fun, it becomes magical.

Children have no idea what is involved when buying a new house. They just see the end picture in mind.

They do not know how much the house costs, or how to get the money to buy it.

They run into the bedrooms and see what their bedroom looks like or what they want their bedroom to look like.

They see the pool and themselves playing in it,

swimming and jumping with their friends and having endless fun!

Whereas adults, we tend to be logical about it all. We think, 'It's going to cost so much money – that I don't have! How am I ever going to be able to afford it? And how will I be able to pay the mortgage?'

If you think it through from a child's perspective, you feel that magic and in that moment anything is possible. Just remember to smile, breathe and have fun. It all goes back to discovering your inner child.

If you think that you do not know how to visualise, or that you cannot visualise, think again. Everyone visualises and I'll prove it: imagine your bathroom in your mind's eye.

Hold that image. Imagine what your bathroom looks like. Imagine walking into your bathroom, switching the light on, and walking to where your toothbrush is.

Pick it up and feel the handle as you hold it in your hand. Feel the texture, and the way it curves in the middle. Now reach for the tube of toothpaste and open it.

Smell its fragrance as you squeeze it onto your toothbrush. Hear the sound of the water as you turn on the tap to wet your toothbrush. Taste the toothpaste as you start brushing your teeth. You come into contact with the cold water as you rinse your mouth.

How does it feel on your skin? Hear the sounds of gargling as you rinse your mouth and spit into the basin. Watch as the water rinses the sink clean. Now you reach for your towel to dry your mouth and hands.

You visualised your bathroom, didn't you? Did you see that? Did you hear that? Did you feel that? You have

Chapter 11: Effortless Results

just visualised! That is how simple it is.

You might think that you have heard it all, that it is all too hard and that it takes too much effort. Just remember, it *is* all about your attitude. Try turning your attitude around. Instead of saying it is too hard, say, 'It's *easy*! I *can* visualise! I *can* do it! I *can* create effortless results! I *can* achieve my goals!'. Just want the change and be the change.

I focus on

∞ Achieving ∞ Visualising ∞ Results

My Thoughts

Effortless Results

My Thoughts

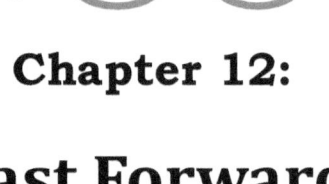

Chapter 12:

Fast Forward

'If you fail to plan, you're planning to fail.'

– Benjamin Franklin

Knowing where you want to go in your life is so much more empowering than just letting your life come to you, not knowing what it's going to dish out next.

If you plan and you know what your next steps are, you can create a very clear vision of your future. You will know that you are moving step by step towards a happy and content life that will cause you to stay on track.

When planning your life, be aware that you might have to adjust it as you grow or as you find that certain things are not going the way you planned. You might put something into practice and then think it is not

Chapter 12: Fast Forward

practical. If this happens, you need to adjust again. Allow yourself to step back, assess, adjust your sails and your direction in life.

Planning allows you the possibility of creating a legacy for your children, family or society once you are no longer in this life.

It allows you to inspire others, because you have created such an amazing life.

The downside of not knowing what those next steps are, or not planning those next steps in your life, may mean you will remain stuck in your past and you might deeply regret this.

You do not want to end up saying, 'I wish I'd done that' or 'if only I hadn't left my job back then' or 'if only I had gone for that new job, I could be so much better off.'

To me, 'fast forward' means not the speed of it, but the consistency of stepping up and out into your future self. How are you going to plan, create and act on your plan?

How consistent are you going to be in creating your future for yourself and your family?

What does your ideal future look like compared to what it looked like in the past or now in the present?

Does it look the same? Does your future look marginally different?

Does it look better?

Considering your next steps and your goals, have you planned them out?

Have you put pen to paper?

Realise that the pen is in your hand – you can create your future.

> 'When the student is ready the teacher will appear.'
>
> **– Unknown**

∞ Look at where you want to be

Pause for a moment and imagine what your life looks like in six months, twelve months, and/or five years from now.

Look at your short-term, medium-term and long-term goals. Ask yourself if you want to be in the same place as you were yesterday or six months ago.

Whenever I go through a rough time in my life, I get to the point where I say, 'That's it, this is enough, no more.'

I need to change something, because I do not want to be here, I want to be somewhere else; I want to create that plan for myself. So, I look at my goals again and readjust them.

∞ How do I want to be?

There is a really great exercise called The Wheel of Life. Used by Life and Business Coaches, The Wheel gives you a snapshot of how your life is at the moment – how balanced it is.

Grab a sheet of paper.

Draw a large circle and segment it into eight equal parts.

Depict these eight areas of your life as it is right now.

Name the segments as follows:

- love & relationships
- finances
- career
- health & wellbeing
- spirituality
- fun & recreation
- personal growth, and
- family & friends.

This wheel can have different segments according to your life. (You can even have a business Wheel of Life, allowing you to separate your segments relating to your business.)

Next, scale the segments from 0–10, starting from the centre of the circle to the outer rim. Zero being the least satisfactory value and ten being the most satisfactory value.

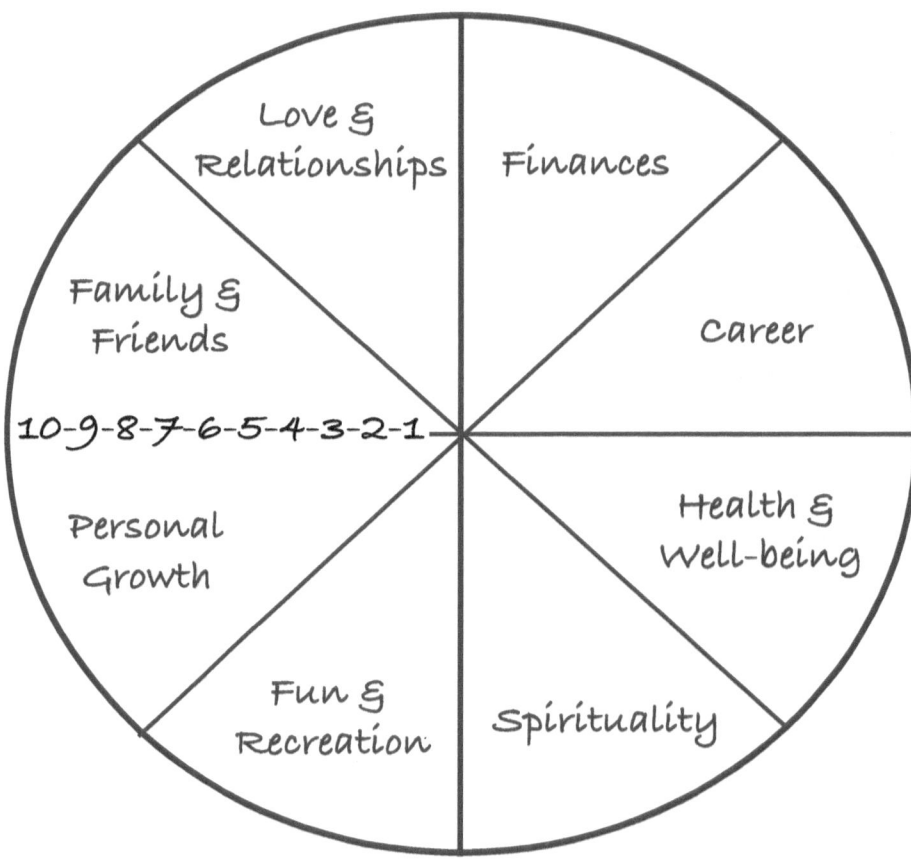

Now, go through each of these sections, asking yourself questions such as:

- 'What is my relationship like?
- How satisfied am I with my relationship?
- Am I putting adequate energy and time into my relationships?
- What do I need?
- What is missing?'

Chapter 12: Fast Forward

Rate your answers on the scale of 1 to 10. Continue with the other areas, asking similar questions for each and rating them accordingly. Once you have rated all the areas, draw a straight or curved line to connect the areas, creating a new perimeter for your Wheel of Life.

You might be surprised after doing this exercise. Ideally, if your life is in total balance, the connected lines should make a complete circle.

Does yours look like this, or is it bumpy and uneven where some areas need a lot of work, while other areas are great? This exercise can be a real eye-opener and great for measuring where you are in life and getting you to think how you can adjust the sails.

I recommend that you do your Wheel of Life every couple of months to assess your progress. See if you can get a smooth line to make your wheel (your life) ideally balanced.

Apply strategies to improve in all areas of your life/wheel. I have included a link to the Wheel of Life on the Resource page.

I have done my Wheel of Life with several of my coaches and was able to get an idea about how balanced (or imbalanced) my life was at the time. I was quite amazed, as I thought I had been cruising along really nicely.

There were areas in my life where I thought, 'Whoa! I thought that I wasn't doing too badly.' I realised then that I should be looking at certain areas in my life to adjust and to plan – like where I want to be in the next five or ten years.

∞ How do I create change?

Something I found to be very helpful was personal development. I immersed myself in it. I read lots of personal development books. There is a myriad of books out there. Some examples are, *The Power of Now,* by Eckhart Tolle and *The Big Leap,* by Gay Hendricks. Reading books such as these will reinforce positivity in your life.

Regular activities like yoga, affirmations and meditation also helped me stay on track. I love listening to empowering CDs on how you can improve your life. One that inspires me time and again is *The Secret* by Rhonda Byrne. You can find this in printed book form, as an audio book and on DVD.

I recently discovered the wealth of personal development video clips on YouTube. I tap into this resource almost every day, in particular, when I need inspiration. Once, whilst doing my ironing (a task I quietly despise ...), I found myself glued on inspirational videos by Lisa Nichols, who featured in *The Secret*. Even if I cannot watch the clips, I can still listen to the tracks – my regular background accompaniment when I am preparing meals for my family! I have included links to Lisa's clips on the Resource page.

Remember to take a holistic approach, rather than a one-sided approach, and be unapologetic in working on your goals. Check in often to see how you are going with your goals. Look at things you need to change or what you need in order to adjust your sails. Above all, keep the faith. Hold on to that picture of what you want and keep tapping into that inner wisdom of knowing where you want to be, what you want to do and who you want to be.

Chapter 12: Fast Forward

Maybe you are not sure what to read, what to watch, what to listen to. There are lots of groups on forum sites and social media, including Facebook, that focus on the topic of personal development and personal growth. You can even seek out blogs on the topic. Working with a coach is a great resource as well, as they keep you accountable. Maybe do a course at your local community hub, or attend one of those conferences I mentioned in an earlier chapter. Personal development seminars are conducted all over the world.

You do not have to do everything all at once. Just be aware that there are so many things out there you can try. I used to do a lot of things at once. Sometimes I would think, 'The more the better', but then it would become all too much; I would be spending too much time trying to keep up with everything.

The reason I included a Resource page on the things that have inspired me and where you can seek information, is to make it easier for you to get to where you need to be. Rather than not knowing where to turn or where to look, it is as easy as going to the back of this book. I hope you find it helpful.

Make it simple, make it easy and make it fun. Also remember to praise yourself for taking that step, for wanting to go 'fast forward' in your life, especially after you have been through a rough time. When you feel that you are in control again after letting yourself fall and creating some action steps, give yourself a pat on the back. Get your support systems in place, and congratulate yourself when you have tapped into your inner being and have seen that breakthrough. Praise yourself and acknowledge yourself for having come this far. Stand tall and be proud!

I want to leave you with an inspiring message from the

great Scottish mountaineer and writer, WH Murray (1913–1996):

> 'Whatever you can do, or dream you can do, begin it. Boldness has genius, power, and magic in it. Begin it now.'

What a fantastic thinking process! It is said that Murray wrote his first book draft as a prisoner of war on rough toilet paper!

Be committed – committed to yourself and committed to your future. Commit yourself to change. By doing this, things will fall into place. Take that step, move towards it and be that mother duck – do not wait for your ducklings to line up. Just move forward and the ducklings will line up and follow.

I focus on

∞ Balance ∞ Simplicity ∞ Commitment

Chapter 12: Fast Forward

'Trust yourself. Create the kind of self that you will be happy to live with all your life. Make the most of yourself by fanning the tiny, inner sparks of possibility into flames of achievement.'

– Golda Meir

Life is a great journey
with the important people in my life

Programs and Offers

Offer 1

Breakthrough to Mastery Session

Have you been having that nagging feeling that something is not quite the way you want it to be in your life?

Are you unsure how to go about discovering what is missing?

Have you been searching for the right strategies to instigate that WOW-Factor?

- Explore what has been holding you back
- Create your crystal clear vision and learn how to set luxuriously luscious goals
- Walk away feeling great, empowered and ready to catapult your life with sure-fire strategies for amazing results.

In just 30 minutes, you can change the way you look at your life.

With a total value of $247, your investment is only $47.

Email support@ruthstuettgen.com with subject line: 'M2M Breakthrough to Mastery'.

(Mention you saw this program offer in this book!)

Offer 2

Ruth as a Speaker

Ruth's keynotes and presentations are inspirational, witty and educational. She has contributed articles to various media outlets and speaks on the following topics:

Business and Marketing for Women in Business
- How to generate all the leads your business can handle
- Everything you've learnt about generating leads and growing your business is wrong

Programs and Offers

- Time Management 101
- 3 Elegant ways to embracing your brand with authenticity.

Women Lifestyle Development
- The WOW-Factor – How You say Yes! to Change
- 7 steps to Freedom
- Blueprint to Navigating from Domestic Violence to Freedom and Empowerment
- The Secret to the Power of Positivity/The Law of Attraction.

Request and check Ruth Stuettgen's availability via email support@ruthstuettgen.com with 'Speaking Request' in the subject line.

Offer 3

Focus on Marketing

Are you looking for ways to balloon your business, be ahead of the game and avalanche your sales?

Have you been burning the candle at both ends to be rich and successful, yet not getting anywhere?

Are you ready to break new ground to control your lifestyle and business?

These packages guarantee acceleration and transformation in both your life and business.

Platinum / Diamond / Gold Focus on Marketing
- 12 months guidance and support (3x weekly / 2x weekly / bi-weekly)
- Unlimited Email access
- Access to cutting-edge online E-Learning System
- Optional Extra with Diamond and Gold package: 12 week *Inspired to Success* personal coaching.

Silver Focus on Marketing
- Weekly group coaching call
- Unlimited Email & E-Learning System access
- 'Buddy System' for accountability
- Optional extra: 12 weeks *Inspired to Success* personal coaching.

Laser Focus Formula for Success

Setting the scene for transformation in 60 minutes, includes:

- Overcoming barriers
- Relationships, health and recreation
- Business and career success.

Email support@ruthstuettgen.com with subject line: 'M2M – B2B Focus Tier Packages'

(Mention you saw this program offer in this book)

The Passion Test

Are you ready for more joy and fulfillment in your life?

Would you like to get really clear on the things that mean the most to you?

Do you want to live a more passionate life?

Getting really clear on your passions – those things that matter most to you – and living them fully, **enhances** so many areas of your life

   Health
      Happiness
         Work
            Family
               Relationships

AND, your passions can act as an 'inner GPS' for the decisions you make in your life. But what if you don't know what they are?

During the simple and powerful 'Passion Test' process you will learn:

- Your top 5 passions – the things that are most important to YOU
- How to align your life with your passions to experience more joy and fulfillment
- Simple strategies to overcome obstacles and challenges which pre-vent you from living your ideal life

- The formula for creating whatever you choose to have in your life
- The one secret to guaranteeing a passionate, meaningful and prosperous life.

Contact Sharon to reserve your appointment – Reg Price $297US. Special HALF OFF for *Misery to Mastery* readers $149US. Price includes two one-hour sessions and 1 followup session.

Sharon Anderson
Passion Test Facilitator
Email: manifestingforlife@gmail.com
www.manifestingforlife.com

A Resource Guide for *Your* Journey

Please feel free to visit my website,
www.ruthstuettgen.com

Domestic Violence Information Websites

How to find out if you are living in a domestic violent situation: http://bit.ly/1AmKn5o

Abuse help agencies in every country in the world and 110 languages: http://www.hotpeachpages.net

Assistance, information and help:
Australia
https://www.1800respect.org.au

Canada
http://womensweb.ca/violence/resources.php

U.S.A
http://www.thehotline.org

Japan
http://www.gender.go.jp/e-vaw/index.html

Cycle of Violence:
www.domesticviolence.org/violence-wheel/

Department of Human Services:
http://www.humanservices.gov.au/customer/subjects/domestic-and-family-violence

Myths and Facts about Domestic Violence:
www.bdvs.org.au/information/myths--facts

Relationships Australia:
http://www.relationships.org.au/

Other Resources

Affirmation Audio: *Sing yourself to Freedom and Empowerment:*
www.ruthstuettgen.com/sing-your-affirmations

Audio: Blueprint for Navigating from Domestic Violence to Empowerment and Freedom:
www.ruthsuettgen.com/audio-DV-Blueprint

Diary Template:
http://www.vertex42.com/calendars/daily-planner.html

www.worksheetworks.com

E-Book: Blueprint for *Navigating from Domestic Violence to Empowerment and Freedom*:
www.ruthstuettgen.com/ebook-DV-Blueprint

Online Dictionary:
http://dictionary.reference.com/browse/dilemma

Steve Pavlina Website on the 400 values:
https://www.stevepavlina.com/articles/list-of-values.htm

The Kelly Services Survey:
http://cnb.cx/1Dn9ax3

http://bit.ly/1EY4vwj

Wheel of Life:
www.ruthstuettgen.com/wheel-of-life

Information Regarding Meditation

Gaia Meditation:
www.ruthstuettgen.com/gaia-meditation

Mindfulness Meditation:
www.kidsmatter.edu.au

Buddhist Meditation:
http://www.wikihow.com/Begin-Zen-Meditation-%28Zazen%29

Health Benefits of Meditation:
www.breath2000.org

http://www.webmd.com/mental-health/features/meditation-heals-body-and-mind

My Inspirations

Below is a list of just some of the books and videos I love, which have inspired me. Some of these I have referenced in this book:

Attwood, Jane – *The Passion Test*
Anjomi, Bijan – *Absolutely Effortless Prosperity*
Branson, Richard – *Screw Business as Usual*
Bristol, Claude and Sherman, Harold – *TNT: The Power Within You*
Byrne, Rhonda – *The Magic*
Byrne, Rhonda – *Hero*
Byrne, Rhonda – *The Secret*
Dalai Lama, His Holiness – *The Art of Happiness*
Dr Chopra, Deepak – *The Higher Self*
Forster, Sandy – *How to be Wildly Wealthy Fast*
Fredrickson, Fabienne – *Embrace your Magnificence*
Hicks, Esther and Jerry – *Ask and it is Given*

Hendricks, Gay – *The Big Leap*
Langemeier, Loral – *Yes! Energy*
Tolle, Eckhart – *Practicing the Power of Now*
Tolle, Eckhart – *The Power of Now*
Vitale, Joe – *Spiritual Marketing*

Video

Nichols, Lisa – *The Art of Holistic Success: Doing Good and Living Epic YouTube Clip*: http://bit.ly/1NCTpn5

www.ingramcontent.com/pod-product-compliance
Lightning Source LLC
Chambersburg PA
CBHW021101080526
44587CB00010B/337